EXPECT THE UNEXPECTED

Facing Mortality Issues With Dignity and Confidence

Written By

WALTER R. PIERCE, Esq.

Bloomington, IN  Milton Keynes, UK

authorHOUSE™

First published by AuthorHouse 2/15/2006

ISBN: 1-4208-8802-1 (sc)

Library of Congress Control Number: 2005908665

*Printed in the United States of America
Bloomington, Indiana*

This book is printed on acid-free paper.

FORWARD

Two hundred years ago, we were lucky to think we'd live to be older than thirty; a hundred years ago, maybe sixty years of age. Today we are looking at seventy-five to eighty years, and in the not so distant future who knows. With longevity comes the time to allow us to increase our wealth and accumulate assets, but with what price – the increased possibility of debilitating injury or infirmity that may render us unable to manage our affairs and make decisions. These unfortunate events catch us at the most inopportune times and leave us powerless to make our feelings and desires known to those around us.

We find that families cannot always agree on what to do, let alone on what they thought their loved one wanted. Look at the Florida case of the woman who went into a coma following a diet which then pitted a spouse against parents – brother against sister – brother against brother – and involved the Governor of Florida, the President of the United States and the Congress of the United States. Think of the stories you've read in the newspapers about persons who remained in a coma for decades. Then there was the recent article about the person who wanted to be cremated, but his family believed such an act would not be in accordance with their religious beliefs on resurrection and wanted to prevent the spouse from complying with her husband's wishes. How many times do parents think their assets will be divided equally among their children, only to find the manner in which they titled those assets dictated a distribution contrary to their wishes. Recently the courts voided charitable designations made by the deceased under a beneficiary designation on a standard form. The deceased designated on the forms that certain organizations should get the proceeds of specified investments, insurance policies and the like. Unfortunately the deceased was hit by a double whammy: state laws generally prohibit charitable organizations from getting more than 25% of the net estate if that person dies within six months of making the designation, and, as to the 25%, the listed organizations were unidentifiable. What do these people all have in common – no advance directives or legally sanctioned provisions that speak for them when they cannot.

This primer is intended to relieve some of the worries such stories create and provide you with the tools necessary to make an informed decision as it may relate to your situation. Make the law work for you, not against you.

Whether you are young or a senior, whether you are male or female, whether you are a professional or blue collar worker, whether you are married, divorced or single, whether you have children or not, whether you are healthy or inflicted with a terminal illness, whether you are a minority, immigrant, or disabled, each of us can find ourselves in the same position – needing someone to make financial and health decisions for us because we cannot. This need does not discriminate. Knowledge of your rights and remedies are essential. This book is vital to your understanding of this critical area of your life.

- the author

CONTENTS

INTRODUCTION

Death and taxes - that's what we learned are the only sure things in life. Sometimes we go to great lengths to try to cheat both of them, only to no avail. Many times our efforts are in vain, not because our intentions are misdirected, but because we do not know the proper format or limitations the law requires. People, in general, don't like to talk about these issues either because they are too complicated, too scary to think about, or just too confusing to comprehend. This primer will take you through a review of the major areas of your lives that many folks take for granted while they are young and which fall off their radar screen as they get older. We will explore these areas together and in plain English. We will group these areas under the concept of "estate planning" (EP) coupled with "advance care planning" (ACP).

ACP is a type of estate and life planning that focuses on issues that need to be considered when a person becomes ill, disabled, incompetent, unconscious or incapacitated. Waiting until one of these events occurs is too late. Health care, financial, memorial and burial decisions will be made by someone whether you did advance planning or not. There are established rules that will be followed in the absence of any specified plans, but those decisions may not be right for you; they may not be the decisions you want made.

Your health care decisions need to be made according to **your** wishes; anatomical gifts should be made **if that is your desire** when you die; bills need to be continuously paid; property interests need to be managed in the cheapest and most efficient manner possible; and funeral and burial arrangements will become necessary. Should it matter if you are unconscious at home, in a hospital emergency room or in the back of an ambulance?

In this book we will concentrate on EP as it relates to your property and assets following your death. Who gets what – relatives, attorneys, the State, charities, friends, the ex who you forgot to take off an insurance policy; who makes the decisions; what is fair; what did the "deceased" intend to happen with the assets accumulated over a lifetime; and, what will actually happen with those assets under the law, because of the lack of planning while the deceased was alive? What happens to the faithful pet which gave unconditional love to its master while such person was alive and competent? A little planning can go a long way.

You can make it easier on everyone, including yourself, by expressing your wishes in a legally acceptable manner. There are several such legally acceptable processes – the will; the trust; powers of attorney; joint titling with rights of survivorship; living wills; pay-on-death or transfer-on-death designations; do not resuscitate orders (DNR); and guardianships. These are the primary methods to use in advance and estate planning. These we will discuss more fully in later chapters.

CHAPTER 1

- Importance of Estate Planning

Estate planning is a mechanism to account for and manage a person's assets during the life of that individual as well as at and after their death. It looks at all sources of wealth to maximize funds available to live on, and the format to pass those assets on to future generations according to your wishes and at the least possible cost and effort. Life and disability insurance policies, annuities, pensions, bank accounts, stocks, bonds, certificates of deposit, real estate holdings, and tangible personal property (automobiles, boats, household goods, jewelry, clothes and the like) account for the bulk of such assets. It allows a person to look at their situation and plan for contingencies down the road. The younger one is at the time they begin such planning, the better able they are to consider alternatives and decide what is in their best interests. However, it is never too late whether you are in your twenties or in your seventies. Estate planning can encompass not only how to accumulate wealth through financial planning for your life goals – paying for college, a house, or retirement – but it also looks to advance care planning in case you become incapacitated, incompetent, ill, unconscious or disabled and plans for disposition of your assets upon your death.

As a youth we think we are invincible, act recklessly at times and only later in life, wonder how we lived so long. Only as we get older do we realize how fragile life can be, and only then do we come to realize the price we are asked to pay for the sins of our youth. In law school we are taught to always consider the possibility there may be that "teenage widow" or "fertile octogenarian". We should concern ourselves with life and death issues regardless of our age, consider what effect they will have on our families and others, and, not the least of which, what their effect will be on us. How will our wishes and concerns be handled if we cannot make our desires known because of some debilitating health condition or death? We all like to think that others will make the right decisions, but that thinking can lead to family disputes, asset depletion and add needless expense to be paid from our estate. To accommodate these concerns the legal profession has come up with several legal devices that can speak for you when you cannot. In this and later chapters we will talk about the living will, the durable health care power of attorney, the durable power of attorney, the will, the living and testamentary trust, the memorial planner, do not resuscitate orders, joint ownership and pay or transfer on death designations. These are documents acceptable under the law to make your decisions just that, yours. They are not without risk and require careful consideration and study. And last, but not the least, let's not forget the family pet. What is to happen to them?

- Protecting Your Assets

All of us have exposure to potential creditors. You may also have exposure due to the assets you own. Perhaps you cannot shovel the sidewalk in front of your home and your neighbor slips and breaks a hip. Perhaps you own a rental property and a pipe breaks, flooding the house and ruining your tenant's furniture as well as your carpeting.

You may have exposure due to your employment. Perhaps you are a physician whose patient has a bad outcome and whose family believes you are responsible. Perhaps you are the accountant who signed off on Enron's books.

You may have exposure from ordinary everyday acts. Perhaps you do not see that a traffic light has turned red and cause an accident. Perhaps you let go of your shopping cart to answer your cell phone and the cart rolls down the hill hitting a baby stroller. Perhaps you are a senior who becomes the target of con artists and others who want to take advantage of your status. You see your nest egg gone in minutes through no fault of your own, other than just getting older and slower and more trusting.

There are a number of ways to manage and minimize these risks. Setting up a corporation or other entity can protect you from personal liability arising from rental property. You can get insurance to protect against the most significant risks. For instance, auto and homeowner's liability insurance can provide insurance up to a certain dollar limit for automobile accidents and home injuries, respectively. An umbrella policy can provide additional coverage for multiple risks, such as home, auto, and other risks. Malpractice insurance can provide protection from workplace-related exposure.

Insurance policies do have limits, which may be exceeded with a serious claim. It becomes important to structure your assets to minimize exposure in the event the policy limits are exceeded or in case you are not insured for the particular risk. State and federal laws allow people to protect some assets from creditors under some circumstances. For instance, creditors may not touch retirement plans such as pensions, 401k accounts, and IRAs to the extent they are reasonably necessary for your support. It may make sense then to fund these accounts as much as possible. Life insurance policies also may be exempt to the same extent. States also typically provide protection for the family home. In some states, such as Florida and Texas, the value of the entire home is protected. In other states, like Ohio, only $5,000 of home equity is protected. Within reason, you can protect assets by placing a non-exempt asset, such as cash, into an exempt asset, such as a retirement account. Real estate may be protected through use of life estates.

Putting some of your assets into family trusts or designating those assets as gifts for children or others may also provide some protection from creditors. However, you must make these gifts far enough in advance so that a creditor cannot make a claim against these assets. Under many state laws, this time period is at least three years out. For these assets to be safe, you typically must make such a gift before you know of, incur, or foresee a creditor's claim. If you do transfer assets after you incur a debt, the length of time a creditor has to make a claim depends on the circumstances of the transfer.

Providing asset protection for your children or others is much simpler than protecting assets for yourself. You can leave the assets in a trust for them and name an independent trustee with the power to make discretionary distributions. Assuming the creation of the trust is not subject to attack by your creditors, your children's creditors would not be able to touch the assets in the trust except in rare circumstances. All these efforts have advantages and disadvantages and are all the more reason for planning.

- Important Terms and Definitions

Administrator – The personal representative of a deceased person appointed by the court to gather assets, pay debts and distribute assets in a case where there is no will; a fiduciary.

Anatomical Gift – A donation of all or a part of the human body to be made upon death.

Attorneys-in-Fact – A person appointed by a third person to act for them when they cannot under a power of attorney.

Beneficiary – Person(s) designated to receive benefits of that person's estate upon the happening of an event, generally death.

Codicil – An amendment to a will, executed under the same state requirements as a will.

Conservator – Person appointed by the court to oversee another's estate because of their age or mental capacity.

Do Not Resuscitate Order - DNR stands for "do not resuscitate." A person who does not wish to have cardiopulmonary resuscitation (CPR) performed may make this wish known through a doctor's order called a DNR order.

Durable Health Care Power of Attorney - An instrument that gives a third party power to make decisions on health care matters specified in the instrument when the maker is unable to do so.

Durable Power of Attorney – An instrument that gives a third party power to make decisions on matters specified in the instrument – generally financial – when the maker is unable or unavailable. When used in conjunction with the Durable Power of Attorney for Health Care, it allows bills to be paid and other business matters to be timely handled during the maker's incapacity, disability or incompetence.

Estate – A term applied to all the property owned or controlled by an individual during their lifetime and at the time of their death.

Executor – The personal representative of a deceased person appointed under a will to gather assets, pay debts and distribute those assets; a fiduciary.

Fiduciary – Persons such as attorneys, executors, trustees, administrators, attorneys-in-fact, or others who act on behalf of third persons.

Grantor – The person who creates a trust agreement and places assets (funding) into the trust.

Guardian – A person appointed by a court to oversee the person and the estate of a minor, or, adult who cannot take care of themselves.

Intestate – The legal status of a person who dies without a will.

Joint and Survivorship – A legal term that identifies the ownership of property as giving each owner an interest according to their proportionate interests while the parties are alive, but distributes the balance of the decedent's share equally to the survivors.

Last Will and Testament – An instrument meeting state requirements for the purpose of distributing a deceased's property, paying debts and providing for any minors upon the death of a person.

Living (*Inter Vivos*) Trust – A trust instrument created during the life of the grantor.

Living Will – An instrument that speaks for an individual that meets certain health conditions when that person cannot speak for themselves.

Next-of-Kin – A blood line or heir by operation of law.

Non-Probate Assets – Assets that are transferred outside a will by operation of law, contract or other instrument.

Pay-on-Death – Like transfer-on-death, it is a designation placed on an account or instrument, such as a bond or stock certificate, that creates a contractual obligation to transfer that account or instrument to the named individual.

Personal Representative – A term referring to a person appointed under a will to see that the assets are gathered, debts paid and distributions made; also called an "executor", if under a will or "administrator", if not.

Per Stripes – A term that allows property to descend by right of representation. A beneficiary's heirs stand in the shoes of the deceased beneficiary.

Pour Over Will – A will that places probate property into a living trust under terms of that living trust.

Probate – The process whereby a will is presented to a court for validation and administration.

Probate Estate – That part of an estate remaining after death that is not transferred by other instruments – trusts, contracts (insurance, POD/TOD).

Powers of Appointment – Rights given by another's will or trust which rights are assignable by will or trust to another.

Residuary Estate – That part of an estate that remains after specific bequeaths and gifts are made; a catchall term to insure all property is disposed following death or funding of a trust.

Settlor – Same as Grantor; a person who creates a trust instrument for a particular purpose and transfers assets into the trust.

Sound Mind and Body – The mental state of a testator necessary to make a valid will; defined generally as knowing the nature and extent of what is owned; understands that the document is a will; and knows who are their family members; it does not mean the person has to be in total possession of their mental faculties.

Statute of Descent and Distribution – A state statute that distributes property according to a fixed method when an individual dies without a will.

Taxable Estate – The entire value of property owned by an individual.

Tenants in Common – A legal term that identifies the ownership of property by giving each owner an undivided interest according to their interests.

Testamentary Trust – A trust instrument created through clauses in a will setting up such an arrangement for some designated purpose whether it be charitable or to provide for the management of assets until some particular event happens, i.e., a minor becomes an adult.

Testate – The legal status of a person who dies having a will.

Testator – The maker of a will; testator refers to a male; testatrix refers to a female.

Transfer-on-Death – A designation placed on an account or instrument, such as a bond or stock certificate, that creates a contractual obligation to transfer that account or instrument to the named individual.

Trust – An instrument that creates an entity separate from the grantor into which property of the grantor is transferred (funding the trust) and which instrument distributes property according to its specific terms. It can be created before death (*inter vivos*) or by will (testamentary).

Trustee – A fiduciary; a person to whom a trust grantor appointed to administer the trust.

Ward – A person for whom the court appointed a guardian.

Will Substitutes – Instruments – e.g., living trusts, contracts – passing title upon death to specified individuals.

- Background Information Necessary

In order to properly assess the necessary legal documents one needs under a particular situation, a person must review their entire estate, determine its value, identify the people and organizations to whom they wish to give their assets and the people they want to entrust with administering their wishes to include personal representatives, trustees, guardians, and attorneys-in-fact.

You should list obvious assets, such as a home or other real estate, savings and checking accounts, investments, 401k accounts, IRAs, pension plans, and insurance policies. You should also itemize valuable personal property, such as jewelry, antiques, collectibles, stamps, rare coins, etc. Ideally, you should photograph and appraise such items as well. This list can serve many purposes. For example, if you have a fire or a burglary, this list and the accompanying photographs and appraisals can help you file a claim with your insurance company.

It is also necessary to identify personal and financial data. This data consists of such information as social security numbers, all bank accounts, safe deposit boxes, addresses of all identified people, dates of birth, and telephone numbers. It is also important to know the sources and location of stocks- bonds- CDs, future inheritances; powers held; pre-nuptials; divorce decrees; locations of all real estate and the nature of its title, mortgages, liens; automobiles; other vehicles and boats; the location of personal household goods; jewelry; and antiques; funeral arrangements; and burial arrangements, to name a few. The depth of such inquiries depends on the detail of effort a person wants to put into the planning of their estate. It sounds like a lot of information, and it is; but laying it all out up front insures the best possible outcome down the road.

Without a complete list of your financial assets, a financial planner cannot know how to change your assets to achieve the proper asset allocation to meet your risk, return, and diversification objectives. Without a complete list of all of your assets, your estate planning professional cannot advise you about taxation issues. Further, without beneficiary designations and titling information, your estate planner cannot help ensure your wishes will be carried out at your death.

Even if your valuables are in a safe deposit box, having a list of such assets will be helpful in the event that there is a delay in finding the key. At least your family will know the contents if there's any urgency about gaining entry to the box. Also, while extremely unlikely, safe deposit boxes have had their contents looted or destroyed.

You may wish to make copies of items you may need in an emergency, such as your durable power of attorney, durable health care power of attorney, living will, and, in many states, your will. Copies of these documents are acceptable for most purposes, and can be kept at home in a safe place. You also may wish to give copies of certain documents (such as your living will and health care power of attorney) to a person named in the document, to a family member, and to your physician or hospital.

o Memorial Service and Burial Planning

Unfortunately, a person's plan for a memorial service, funeral service and burial or cremation cannot be legally enforced. However, a person is not without recourse or tools to make those plans more likely to be implemented than not.

Pre-paying for funeral and cremation services, purchasing burial plots and contracting for perpetual care can make following a person's wishes less difficult and expensive. Certainly, though, if family members have some personal religious or other reason to avoid the contract you made, there is little anyone can legally do. Normally under state law, the spouse or, in lieu of such, the next of kin will be given authority to make the ultimate decision.

One need only to look to recent newspaper articles to see these issues – one such article recently reported on the deceased's family that disagreed with the spouse on whether the deceased ought to be cremated or buried. The family believed cremation would preclude resurrection on judgment day according to the tenants of their beliefs. Who should prevail: the deceased's stated wishes – the spouse – the family? Having pre-paid arrangements already in-place increases the likelihood those wishes will be followed in the event of any disagreement.

Only by adequately exploring these issues with loved ones, attaching any pre-arrangement contracts to a memorial planning document and giving that plan to a trusted person can one feel relatively certain their wishes will be adhered to at death. A sample of a simple memorial planning document is found in Appendix A.

Generally, a pre-arranged funeral contract refers to the purchase of funeral goods and services before they are needed from a local funeral home. Nationally, approximately one-third of funerals are arranged and purchased ahead of time. Similar contracts can be made with cemeteries for the actual burial site, preparation and perpetual care of that site. The cemetery cannot force you to purchase memorials from them, although they may have regulations governing size, placement and the like.

➤ Pre-Arranged Funeral

Pre-arrangement allows an individual to talk directly to the funeral director about his or her own funeral preferences. Also, it can relieve surviving family members of financial burdens and from having to make funeral decisions while grieving. Finally, individuals who currently qualify for Medicaid assistance or who anticipate qualifying may pre-pay their funerals without impacting their Medicaid eligibility.

By pre-paying, you are tying up your funds. Additionally, if you cancel the pre-paid contract, you may not receive all of the funds back from the funeral home. The funeral home will use the pre-paid money either to buy an insurance policy on the contract beneficiary's life or place the funds in trust. In the case of an insurance policy, the pre-paid funds are used to purchase a single-pay policy that has a built-in growth factor. When the contract beneficiary dies, the insurance policy proceeds are paid to the funeral home to cover the cost of the beneficiary's funeral.

If the pre-paid funds are placed in a trust, state law, such as is in effect in Ohio, requires that 100 percent of pre-arrangement funds be placed into the trust together with all interest generated by the trust funds. The funeral home may not access those trust funds until the contract beneficiary dies and the funeral services are performed. Under the law, the financial institution may not pay the funds to the funeral home until it receives a death certificate and proof that the funeral services have been provided.

Pre-arranged contracts may either be revocable (can be canceled) or irrevocable (cannot be canceled). For the first seven days after the contract is signed, however, the consumer may revoke **any** pre-arranged contract— even an irrevocable one. During the first seven days, the consumer is entitled to a full refund. After this initial cancellation period expires, a consumer can cancel only a "revocable" contract. If the revocable pre-arranged contract guarantees the price of the funeral, the consumer is entitled to receive back from the funeral home 80 percent of the principal and 90 percent of the interest earned by the trust. If the pre-arranged contract does not guarantee a price, the consumer will get back 100 percent of all principal and interest when he or she cancels the contract.

An individual can have only minimal resources in order to qualify for Medicaid benefits. An irrevocable pre-paid funeral contract does not count as a resource, and therefore does not disqualify the individual from receiving Medicaid assistance.

A guaranteed price contract means that the funeral home guarantees to provide you with the funeral goods and services you selected for the amount of money stated in the contract. This means that you or your estate will not be required to pay any additional cost for the guaranteed items.

If the contract does not guarantee the prices charged, the price of the funeral will be determined at the time the services and merchandise are provided. Any amount you pre-pay will be considered as a deposit to be applied toward the purchase price. However, if the original money paid on the contract plus the interest earned on those funds are not sufficient to cover the price of the funeral goods and services, you or your estate will be responsible for the difference.

If you are interested in a pre-arranged contract, you should carefully consider asking the funeral director the following questions:

(a) Where will the pre-arranged funds be deposited until they are needed?

(b) Will I receive verification from the financial institution that the prepaid funds have been deposited in the trust account?

(c) If the funds are used to purchase an insurance policy, will I receive verification that the policy has been purchased?

(d) What items in the contract, if any, are covered by a price guarantee?

(e) Is the pre-arranged contract irrevocable or revocable?

(f) If the contract is revocable, how can I cancel the contract?

> ➤ Pre-Arranged Burial

In many states, all cemeteries, except for private family cemeteries or cemeteries in which there have been no burials during a period of years (typically 25 years), must be registered with the State. In Ohio, for example, the Division of Real Estate of the Ohio Department of Commerce maintains such registry. To be a private family cemetery it must, of course, be one containing human remains; with at least three-fourths of those whose remains are buried there having a common ancestor or must be the spouse or adopted child of that common ancestor. Regardless, not all cemeteries are perpetual care cemeteries.

A perpetual care cemetery is a cemetery that has an endowment trust fund. This fund provides annual income for the upkeep of the cemetery. Under state law, most cemeteries typically are required to place ten (10) percent of the revenue generated by lot sales and sales of mausoleums into a trust fund. The cemetery may draw off the income and interest earned by the trust fund on an annual basis to offset cemetery maintenance and repair costs. However, family cemeteries, and cemeteries that are owned and operated exclusively by churches, religious societies, established fraternal organizations, or the city, state or federal government, are not required to have endowment care funds. Consumers should check with the cemetery and ask if it has an endowment care trust.

State law does not require cemeteries to buy back grave plots and mausoleum spaces that they do not need. Always check with the cemetery prior to buying a lot to see if they will buy it back, sell the lot to another buyer for you, or allow you to exchange the lot for another space in the cemetery. Situations change. When you were born your family may have wanted you to be buried in the family cemetery where their parents and grandparents were buried; but then you got married, had a family and moved far away. You decide to buy your own family plot in your new location. Your spouse then dies and you get remarried to a person who has their own children. You now have a blended family of several distinct families. What do you do with the plots you originally bought with the first spouse?

These are issues you need to think about, but were not contemplated earlier.

Buyers are free to purchase monuments and markers from independent monument companies and funeral homes. However, the cemetery may impose restrictions on the size and type of monuments and markers they will allow in the cemetery. Be sure to check before pre-paying for a monument.

An outer burial container is a vault or grave liner into which the casket is placed when it is interred. The purpose of the outer burial container is to prevent the ground from caving in around the casket and creating depressions above ground. The law does not require the use of an outer burial container, but many cemeteries do require that grave liners or burial vaults be used to prevent graves from sinking in.

Under many state laws, including Ohio, a cemetery may only charge for its actual services and expenses in installing burial vaults. Therefore, imposing a penalty on a buyer who purchased a vault from a source other than a cemetery is generally illegal.

Check to see if the state in which you are to be buried has an alternate dispute resolution mechanism. In Ohio, the Ohio Cemetery Dispute Resolutions Commission has the authority to resolve complaints levied against **registered** Ohio cemeteries. The Commission tries to resolve these complaints through mediation. If the Commission or the Division of Real Estate believes that a cemetery has violated the law, it will refer the complaint to the prosecutor's office in the county where the cemetery is situated or to the Ohio Attorney General's Office.

o   Health and Dementia Issues

Nobody ever expects the unexpected? This seems like a dichotomy of terms. Yet that is what pre-planning attempts to anticipate. A person goes too far with their diet and slips into a perpetual coma. A mother goes on life support while carrying a baby after having suffered a stroke that made her brain dead in order to bring the baby to full term. You or a loved one is involved in an accident and becomes a quadriplegic. As you age, you may contract Alzheimer's; you may suffer mini-strokes; or dementia may rob you of your mind and memory. Who will make decisions with regard to your medical care? Should you be put on life support indefinitely; should you be resuscitated if your heart fails; and should your organs be donated upon your death? These are decisions that have to be made by someone. These decisions can and will cause anguish among and between family members and your spouse. Do you need a guardian, conservator, or attorney-in-fact to manage your affairs while you cannot, even if you are lucid? What are your choices? What are the benefits and pitfalls of those choices? We will look at these choices in future chapters.

Like health care matters, some states, including Ohio, passed legislation creating a "Declaration of Mental Health Treatment", a document that allows individuals to state their own preferences regarding mental health treatment and to appoint a person to make mental health care decisions for them when they are unable to do so. These declarations will be discussed in a later Chapter.

    o   Estate Information

As we said earlier in this book, a complete disclosure of one's estate allows the professional planner to assess the best mechanisms available to protect those assets; provide for their disposition upon your death; and to avoid the payment of taxes, whether they are income, gift or estate taxes. To accomplish this disclosure, many estate planning professionals prepare a questionnaire to elicit this information. A sample questionnaire is found in Appendix B and will assist you in identifying those assets. Generally there are five reasons to plan your estate.

1. Name guardians for minor children.

You can only nominate guardians for your minor children in a properly drawn will. Without adequate provision in a will, a probate court will decide what is in the best interests of the children. Can you see battling grandparents? Is the surviving spouse a step-parent, not having adopted the children? Who do you think knows the best placement for your children – you or the court?

2. Choose the timing and specify desired distributions.

Disinheriting your children when there is a surviving spouse can be critical. Otherwise, assets belonging to the children by virtue of inheritance may have to be managed by someone and protected through the probate court until they reach the age of majority. Real property gets tied up and can make its sale more complicated. There are good reasons you may not, though, want property to pass to your spouse. If you have a blended family, there may be reasons to by-pass the surviving spouse and leave property to the children. You will want to explore all the ramifications of such bequeaths when you prepare your will. Do not assume your beneficiaries or state law will necessarily follow your wishes.

Even if your children are of legal age, often it is a good idea not to leave assets outright to your "younger" beneficiaries. By holding these assets in trust, you can protect those assets from your beneficiaries' creditors and future ex-spouses. You can mete out the assets over time so that your beneficiaries can get maximum use of those assets without the opportunity to squander them.

3. Make provisions for heirs with special needs.

By planning effectively, you can decide how your assets will help your special needs heirs while not disqualifying them from receiving government assistance such as Medicaid. Many of these individuals are living longer and may well out-live their parents. By creating a properly written special needs trust, you may be able to provide security for both you and your children.

4. Choose who will make decisions for you when you cannot.

People often think that estate planning only includes planning for what happens after you die. However, a major part of estate planning deals with what will happen if you become incapacitated, ill, incompetent, unconscious or disabled. Who will make financial and health care decisions for you?

5. Seek tax reductions where possible.

Proper estate planning may reduce state and federal estate taxes. States have set limits where estates are not taxed. In Ohio that limit is $338,333. There are no federal estate taxes for estates less than $1.5 million in 2005. If your estate is more than this, consideration of these taxes may be important when weighed against what you want to do with your assets. There are also income tax considerations to account for if any of your assets are income producing, such as stocks, rental property, bank accounts and the like. Carefully consider the total costs and risks of transferring those assets into shelters when compared to the actual taxes owed before acting. There is a myth out there that the state and federal government gets the bulk of your estate when you die. For most of us they will get little or none.

In the next chapter we will look into the various legal documents available to protect your assets and to help ensure that your wishes are followed whether you are disabled, incompetent, incapacitated, unavailable, unconscious, or, when the time comes, deceased.

CHAPTER 2

- The Trust Agreement

Trusts can be useful for protecting and transferring your assets, both before your death as well as after your death. Basically you are creating a separate legal entity, placing all or some of your assets into that trust (called funding the trust), appointing someone or some company (either a bank or trust company) to administer the trust and thereby removing those assets from probate. Your need to be involved on a day-to-day basis is eliminated unless you are the trustee. In other words, you can delegate authority to others to deal with your assets. Of course you can also designate yourself as the trustee with another person to succeed you if you become unable under whatever conditions you specify.

Likewise, if you have minor children or children with special needs, or even parents with special needs, having a trust created upon your death by way of a will (commonly referred to as a "Testamentary Trust") may afford you some comfort to know that your assets are protected for the benefit of those beneficiaries when you no longer can be involved. Trusts can be revocable or irrevocable. There are advantages to both, but there are also disadvantages. The greatest disadvantage is that assets are no longer yours in an irrevocable trust.

o   The Living Trust

A "living" trust is one that can be amended and revoked by the person creating the trust (the "grantor"). It is called an *"inter vivos"* trust. The benefit of this trust is that the grantor keeps all the benefits of the property placed into the trust. The terms of the living trust are established in a written agreement signed by the grantor and the trustee, and spell out what happens to the trust property both during the grantor's life and following their death. Frequently, grantors serve as their own trustee during the grantors' lifetime. Tax liability generally remains with the grantor because it is revocable. An outline sample of a living trust is set forth in Appendix C.

o   Avoiding Probate

One common goal of many people is to avoid "probate". A living trust's assets do not go through probate, but pass directly to intended beneficiaries upon the grantor's death according to the terms of the trust. If a grantor's purpose in creating a living trust is to avoid probate, then the grantor must remember to transfer ownership and title to all existing and future assets into the living trust. Any assets not placed in the trust or designated to pass to the trust on death will go through probate and be disposed of by a will, if one exists. Thus, even if you create a trust, it is highly recommended to also have a will. If you intend for the trust to continue after your death, then your will should have "pour-over" clauses, i.e., provisions that will allow the probate assets to move (pour-over) into the living trust..

o   Saving Taxes

It is a common misconception that avoiding probate avoids estate taxes. A taxable estate may or may not equate with the probate estate. Whether it does or not is not relevant to the issue of taxes. Estate taxes are taxes assessed on all the assets owned by the deceased at the time of death unless these assets were placed into some form of tax exempt status (like placing ownership through a title transfer into the beneficiary's name reserving a life estate for yourself while you were alive). Seeking advice from a tax professional is recommended because many such transfers are in essence gifts and can invoke the gift tax laws. The old saying goes: "you cannot avoid death and taxes." But we keep trying.

As a revocable trust the income of the living trust will be taxed to the grantor just as if the trust did not exist for income tax purposes. After the death of the grantor, the trust may be taxed at rates that are higher than individual rates, unless the assets are transferred to the beneficiaries during the taxable year. Upon death the trust takes on a life entity of its own.

Reports as to the demise of the federal estate tax are somewhat exaggerated. During the period beginning January 1, 2002, and continuing through December

31, 2009, the federal estate tax remains in existence. During that time, the amount that a person can pass free of federal estate taxes, other than amounts that qualify for the marital or charitable deductions, rise in stages from its current level of $1.5 million (2004 and 2005), to $2 million (2006 through 2008), and finally $3.5 million (2009). During the same period, the maximum estate tax rate will decline gradually from the current level of 60 percent to 45 percent.

On January 1, 2010, if Congress does not act to change the law before that time, the federal estate tax will be repealed. At that time there will be no federal estate tax on assets you may pass on to your beneficiaries. If Congress does not act, though, the estate tax laws will go back to their original status pre-2000. Many folks doubt Congress will allow that to happen, but with the current deficit, Congress may settle on something in-between by setting a high dollar exemption rather than eliminating the tax altogether. This uncertainty should not dissuade you from any estate planning, only to consider the possibilities and monitor any Congressional action.

Under the current law, in 2010, your beneficiaries will no longer be able to inherit the assets with a "step-up" in the income tax basis (an adjustment that allows you to use as a basis of valuing the asset as the time of death rather than the time the deceased purchased the asset). The advantage to inheriting assets with an unlimited "step-up" in income tax basis is that you avoid tax on any appreciation in the assets between the date of purchase and the date of death.

This can represent significant savings for assets that have been owned for a long period of time. For example, your parents bought a house years ago for $100,000; at the time of their death it is worth $500,000. Currently estate taxes are valued on the $500,000 value and you inherit the property at the $500,000 value. If you sell the house there are no capital gains on the difference of $400,000. However in 2010, there are no estate taxes and your capital gains on the sale will include the $400,000 in appreciated value. Currently there are also limitations on the step-up of assets.

Under federal law, the step-up in income tax basis is limited to $1.3 million of appreciation when assets are passed on to someone other than a spouse, and to $3 million of appreciation when assets are passed to a spouse. Under law, beneficiaries might have to report capital gains when they sell inherited assets by referring to the decedent's original cost basis. Taxpayers will be required to keep careful records of tax basis (i.e., receipts, purchase orders, purchase agreements, etc.) so that their heirs will know how to calculate the tax basis when they inherit the assets and so that they can establish the basis for the Internal Revenue Service. The same will be true in 2010.

o   Advantages of Trusts Over Probate

Privacy. The terms of a living trust are contained in a private document, while the terms of a will, including beneficiary designations, become a matter of public record upon the grantor's death, and after the will has been filed with the probate court.

Control. A trustee of a living trust has more independence and control than an executor of a will because, unlike an executor, the trustee is not required to file a trust or any other reports with a court.

Lower costs. A living trust avoids the costs of the probate process, which typically include court costs, appraisal fees, executor's commissions and attorney fees.

Speed of transfer. A trustee could begin making distributions of assets to beneficiaries soon after the grantor's death.

Avoidance of multiple probate proceedings. If homes or other real estate are owned in a number of different states, a living trust may be used to avoid separate probate proceedings in two or more states. But remember, the assets must have been placed in the trust while you were alive.

       o   Disadvantages of the Trust

Lifetime effort. Implementing a funded living trust is likely to be more time consuming and tedious than drafting a will. It will certainly take additional time to re-title property such as automobiles and real estate both in preparation of documents as well as filing those documents.

Lifetime Costs. The cost of making and maintaining a living trust during an individual's lifetime generally costs more than a will. You should take into consideration the higher initial costs of establishing a trust, the continuing costs to administer the trust, those costs needed to transfer assets into the trust and the costs to terminate the trust upon the death or other conditions.

Absence of court review. The administration of a living trust will not be supervised by any court, increasing the possibility of incorrect administration by the trustee, whether intentional or unintentional.

o   The Grandchildren

You gave your children a great start in life and hopefully, they are all well established. Leaving them your assets to ensure their security later in life may not be the best use of your assets. What about your grandchildren? Would you like to secure their future as well? It may be easier than you think.

You can give $11,000.00 to each grandchild each year with no gift or estate tax consequences with a lifetime limit of $1,000,000.00. If you are married you can give twice this amount. Due to the miracle of compound interest, this can create quite a nest egg by the time the grandchild is at retirement age. The average rate of return for large, publicly-traded stocks has been about 7.3 percent. Money invested at this rate would double about every ten (10) years. Let's say you and your spouse each contribute $11,000 for the first two years of a grandchild's life, for a total of $44,000. If this nest egg were invested and returned at the average historical stock market rate of return, by the time each of your grandchildren is age 52, they would have over $1.4 million in today's dollars. By age 62, the earliest age to begin drawing social security, they would have over $2.8 million.

Of course, when your grandchild is a newborn, you cannot just give that child a check. However, you can set up an irrevocable trust with your grandchild as the beneficiary. In fact, you can set up one trust for all of your grandchildren that will split into separate trusts after your death or when each grandchild has reached a certain age. You can set up the standards for distributions and you can ensure that the nest egg is not squandered by your grandchildren before they are mature enough to handle the responsibility. Tax liability will be with the trust.

As with most things there are downsides to setting up irrevocable trusts for your grandchildren. First, you cannot revoke the trust if you find you need the principal. The assets belong to the beneficiaries; you no longer own them. You have to be careful that the trust assets will not be subject to a "generation-skipping transfer (GST) tax." The GST tax applies whenever you give assets to someone that is two or more generations younger than you are. The GST tax is in addition to the normal estate tax, and the rate is between 45 percent and 55 percent, depending upon the year of the transfer. However, you and your spouse can each give at least

$1.1 million to your grandchildren without paying the GST tax. Also, a variety of techniques can be used to pass assets for the benefit of your grandchildren without paying the GST tax.

- The Will

  o Who and How of Wills

The Last Will and Testament is by far the most recognized document by which people wish to distribute their property after their death. The will is, in fact, only one type of document that speaks for you at the time of your death. The will is intended to tell your family how you want your possessions and money to be distributed. It becomes a public document when it is filed with the probate court and its implementation will be under court direction. To be valid the will must comply with state law. Generally that requires the will be in writing, signed at the end by the person desiring to make the will and who must be over 18 years of age, and witnessed by two disinterested persons also over the age of 18, all of whom declare that the document purports to be the last will and testament of that person. A sample will outline is found in Appendix D.

  o Pitfalls

What is probate property that passes under a will? Were the witnesses present at the time you executed the will? Did they believe you to be of sound mind and did they understand that the document was in fact your last will? Did the testator and witnesses sign the will at the end? Because you will not be available to answer these questions as might not your witnesses also, it is advisable to have a will prepared by an attorney. For one thing, the law generally presumes a will written by an attorney is in fact compliant with the law and the attorney can testify as to the facts of execution, if necessary. The attorney generally cannot testify as to the contents of the will under attorney-client privilege constraints.

    o   Will vs. Will Substitutes

If your assets are covered by a will substitute why worry about having a will? In short you shouldn't have to. But if the substitute fails and you do not have a will, your property may not go to the individuals or organizations you want. Having a will covers you in those cases where you let these will substitutes lapse or they are found invalid. Further, the courts may not find the manner in which you titled property to really be a will substitute? For instance, you hold property jointly without more. Under the common law and more recently by statute, such titling really becomes a tenancy in common. This means one-half or some proportionate share will not pass directly to the other joint owner but be part of your estate. The law requires such joint title to include additional words "with right of survivorship" in order to be a will substitute and thus pass your interest to the other joint owner(s) directly without going through the court process.

    o   Disposition of Property

Generally we all own certain types of property and may have other types of assignable rights that need to be disposed of somehow – real property, tangible personal property, intangible personal property and "powers of appointment". A person may dispose of these rights and property in any manner they want and generally to whomever they want. The laws of the various states do limit this right somewhat by reserving certain interests of spouses and minor children to claim property against the will. The nuances of these laws need to be explained to you by an attorney depending on your particular situation. Many people believe that to disinherit a child you need to at least leave them $1.00; likewise a spouse. All you really need to do to disinherit a child is to make it known by the language in the will that you know they exist and intentionally make no provision for them. You can try to do this with a spouse, but without a prenuptial agreement, state laws generally allow a spouse to elect certain rights against the will. In other words she can take what was left to her under the will or elect to take her statutory share, which generally amounts to that share she would take had there been no will.

o   Dying Without the Will

If a person dies without a will, the law refers to the person as dying intestate. In those cases the state statute makes the distribution under what is commonly referred to as the "statute of descent and distribution". This statute fixes a formula for distribution to your nearest family members. You have no say in the matter; the law controls. So if you have a spouse and children, your property may be divided at the time of your death between your spouse and the children, rather than to the spouse alone. That can complicate matters tremendously, especially with the sale of real property and if those children are minors.

If these children are minors, a guardian will have to be appointed to manage and sign off on any transfers. Your spouse may or may not be the guardian of that property and whoever is appointed guardian will have to pay for and provide a surety bond covering the management of that property until the children are 18 years of age. Furthermore, someone will have to be appointed as an "administrator" in order to gather the assets, prepare the forms to be filed with the probate court, file tax returns and distribute the assets. Dying without a will can get to be expensive, probably more so than if you have a will considering that under a will you can waive bonding, take advantage of marital deductions and make charitable contributions.

- The Trust Within the Will or Pour-Over Will

  o Pour-Over Will

As described above, the two most prevalent documents used to manage assets are the living trust and will. With the former, a person has placed their assets into a trust for purposes of management and upon their death to either distribute the property outright or continue the trust for the foreseeable future. But suppose there is property that belongs to the decedent but is not part of the trust for whatever reason. Suppose the desire of the decedent is to place that property into the trust after their death and then have that trust continue for some period of time. How can this be accomplished? Call on the pour-over will.

Basically such a will contains provisions that will transfer specific, certain or all the probate property into this trust for distribution to named individuals according to the terms of the trust. Some sample provisions are found in Appendix E. These clauses are useful when you think all your assets are in the trust, but your heirs find out only after your death they are not. The pour-over clauses transfer that property into your trust rather than distributing the property directly to your beneficiaries.

o   The Testamentary Trust

Suppose you do not believe your spouse or children can handle an outright gift upon your death, but you do not want to go to the expense of setting up a living trust. Even if your children are adults, maybe you feel they may squander all their inheritance while they are young. Maybe your spouse has no money management abilities or doesn't want that responsibility. What can you do?

Consider creating a testamentary trust in your will. Such a trust operates similar to a living trust except it activates only upon your death. If you revoke your will, no such trust comes into being unless added to your new will. Basically all probate property falling under the will is placed in a trust defined by the terms of the will. The trust then operates to manage the assets of the estate for the term of the trust. The main difference between the living trust and the testamentary trust is that the latter will be under the supervision of the probate court for as long as the trust exists. That means periodic reporting and accounting to the court, probably on an annual basis. It may mean securing court approval for certain transactions which are unlike the living trust which operates without court supervision. Sample outlined provisions for the creation of a testamentary trust are found in Appendix F.

Chapter 3 will look into other forms of will substitutes than trusts. They are more simplistic to create and implement than trusts, but have their own risks. Property will pass under the designation selected rather than how you may actually want to distribute the property at the time of your death. One tends to forget how they designated the disposition of the property until it is too late. Also the reason for the designation may change. You may remarry; or, the designated beneficiary may die. You must consider these factors when you choose such will substitute.

CHAPTER 3

- Will Substitutes Other Than Trusts

Assets that are owned jointly with rights of survivorship (such as bank accounts, a house or car), or assets that name beneficiaries (such as life insurance, annuities, POD and TOD accounts), also will pass upon death to the survivor or beneficiary, and will not be probate assets. These are typically called will substitutes.

  o Joint Ownership With Rights of
     Survivorship

Almost all joint bank accounts have a survivorship feature. This means that following the death of one of the holders (or depositors) of a joint account, the account automatically passes to the other holder or holders. This is an easy method of estate planning and the reason for the popularity of such accounts. For example, a parent can open a joint and survivorship account with a child as the joint owner and know the child will have the account at the parent's death.

According to many states' law, it is presumed that, during the lifetime of the parties to the account, the account belongs to all of them according to the contributions of each. States' laws presume that after the death of the depositor, the assets in a joint and survivorship bank account go to the other holder(s). For many years, however, the law allowed an interested person to prove by clear and convincing evidence that the depositor actually intended the account to benefit someone other than the joint account holder(s). Clear and convincing is a high standard to meet. Expressing a desire to the joint holder to distribute the funds to all their siblings is insufficient to meet this burden, even if the joint owner acknowledged this request.

Many states like Ohio have reinforced this position by court decision. In 1994, the Supreme Court of Ohio held that the way in which a bank account is opened is conclusive. In other words, the intention of the depositor is determined only by the form of account chosen: ownership of a joint account created in survivorship form will be automatically transferred to the survivor.

Conversely, ownership of a joint account which does not provide for survivorship will not be transferred to the survivor, but will become part of the deceased depositor's estate to the extent that the depositor contributed to the account. Only where there is evidence that the depositor did not freely intend to establish the account (for example, evidence of fraud, duress, undue influence, or lack of mental capacity on the part of the depositor) will a court now consider distributing the account assets in a way not consistent with the form of the account.

That decision makes these accounts easier to administer, but also requires consumers to know more about the legal effects of joint and survivorship accounts. The person (for example, your son) added to the bank account becomes a legal owner of the funds. Such a survivorship bank account many times is set up for convenience, such as, for example, naming one child as a joint party so that an elderly parent's bills can more easily be paid by the child. However, the account will now will be owned by that child alone upon the parent's death, even though the parent may have intended the account to be distributed among several children. Also, the son can make deposits and withdrawals from the account or use your money to pay his bills. His creditors can attach the account to satisfy his debts. The child may promise to split the account with the other siblings when the parent dies, but if the child decides not to share, there is nothing anyone can do about it.

If you are a single and older individual without children or siblings, you may set up a joint account with a neighbor to pay bills. Sounds okay, but is it safe. Recognize if your neighbor has credit problems, you risk losing your money to your neighbor's creditors. What if your neighbor is sued for divorce? Your joint account could be tied up in those proceedings. Also, do you intend for your neighbor to have your money when you die?

In an effort to help consumers become aware of the legal effects of joint and survivorship accounts, some states have adopted legislation called the Uniform Multiple Persons Account Act. It has been adopted in states other than Ohio. Under this law, bankers are required to more completely disclose the legal consequences of joint and survivorship accounts.

As a person grows older, the idea of adding the name of a friend or relative to a house deed, in addition to a bank account, may appear attractive for the same reasons talked about above. For example, you may want to avoid probate or ensure that someone can handle finances in the event of illness. These goals are worthwhile, but disadvantages should also be considered before adding a person's name to a bank account or deed.

Dealing with real property takes on special consideration. Like bank accounts, once you add another person's name (for example, your sister's) to your house deed, she has the same legal rights to the property as you had as sole owner. In fact, she could move in or sell her portion of the property. She could also prevent you from selling the house in the future. She could mortgage her part of the residence or her creditors could place a lien against the property. Finally, should you decide to transfer title wholly to another person, that person could legally evict you. The property would then be solely her property.

Since there are many alternatives available, both to protect your interests and to satisfy your goals, discuss the options with a professional and be sure you fully understand the implications of adding a friend or relative to your home deed or bank account. There are several ways to meet your goals without placing yourself at risk

o   Pay-on-Death/ Transfer-on-Death

Alternative bank account formats can help you achieve your goals while protecting your interests. For instance, a "payable on death" (POD) bank account allows you to direct bank funds to a specific individual upon your death, but does not allow that individual or their creditors to use or attach the funds during your lifetime.

If you wish someone to receive the account upon your death, and you wish to avoid probate, simply make the account POD. The account will still be paid at death, but during your lifetime, only you have any rights to the account. With a POD account, you keep control, you still avoid probate, and you minimize the risk.

Many state laws, including Ohio, allow individuals of modest means, who do not need the tax benefits of a trust, to avoid probate on their real estate by creating a Transfer-On-Death (TOD) Deed. A TOD Deed is simply a real estate deed with a special provision allowing the property owner to directly transfer the ownership of real estate at the owner's death to whomever the owner designates by name. The TOD Deed permits the direct transfer of the described property to the designated beneficiary upon the death of the owner after a death certificate and an affidavit are filed in the Recorder's office by a designated beneficiary. However, a TOD

Deed does not eliminate any estate taxes that otherwise would have been payable.

Further, the designated beneficiary has no rights during the owner's lifetime. The law specifically provides that a TOD Deed has no effect on the present ownership of real property, and a person designated as a TOD beneficiary has no interest in the real property until the death of the owner of the interest.

The law permits the designation of "one or more other persons identified in the deed by name". Because individuals must be named, a designation of "my children" would not be valid. A contingent TOD beneficiary can be designated. For example, the TOD beneficiary could be "Sally Doe, if living; otherwise William Doe." If no named beneficiary is living, the real estate becomes part of the owner's probate estate.

o   Designation of Beneficiaries

There are many instances where you are faced with a contract asking you to name beneficiaries. These principally include retirement plans, life insurance policies and annuities. A beneficiary designation is a document that identifies who is to receive the proceeds upon your death. Most beneficiary designations allow the owner to select a primary beneficiary and a contingent beneficiary. The primary beneficiary receives the proceeds upon the death of the owner. The contingent beneficiary receives the proceeds if the primary beneficiary is not living. Generally, there are no restrictions on who can be named as a beneficiary.

Most commonly, people name one or more individuals including a spouse or children, a trust, or a charity as their primary and contingent beneficiaries.

There are considerations to keep in mind when completing beneficiary designations. Suppose you recently remarried and updated your will to leave everything that you own to your current spouse. Years ago, you signed a beneficiary designation for your 401(k) plan and designated your former spouse as the primary beneficiary. Should you update that beneficiary designation to match your new will?

Of course you should. It is important to understand that a beneficiary designation may override wills, trusts, and other estate planning documents. If there is conflict between a beneficiary designation and a will, the beneficiary designation may prevail under state law. In the case described, even though you have updated your will, if you fail to update the beneficiary designation, your former spouse may receive the proceeds upon your death according to the contract.

There can also be a multitude of tax problems using beneficiary designations. For example, a common tax problem is having life insurance proceeds payable to your estate. Life insurance proceeds generally pass free of state estate tax to beneficiaries other than to your estate. However, if you fail to name a beneficiary on your beneficiary designation or if all of the beneficiaries that you name have predeceased you, the life insurance proceeds will be paid to your estate and will be subject to state estate tax.

    o   Life Estates

Perhaps you want to gift your house to your beneficiary and take it out of probate, but still want to live in the house until you die. This is accomplished by reserving a life estate in you and gifting the balance to your beneficiaries as remaindermen. While a life estate does not fully protect your home from the pitfalls discussed earlier, it gives you the legal right to live in the home for the remainder of your life.

- Powers of Attorney

If you wish someone to help with paying your bills, give that person a limited power of attorney for the account. A power of attorney is a document whereby an individual, known as the "principal," appoints another individual, known as the "attorney-in-fact," to make financial and business decisions for the principal. This should not be confused with a "durable health care power of attorney" that appoints another individual to make health care treatment decisions for a principal if the principal is unable to make his or her own decisions. There are several types of powers of attorney – special or limited, general and durable.

A "power of attorney" bank account, for instance, enables another person to handle your financial affairs in the event you cannot do so yourself, but the account does not have to pass to that person upon your death. A power of attorney account does not entitle the person

EXPECT THE UNEXPECTED

or their creditors to personally use or attach the funds during your lifetime.

When powers of attorney begin depends upon the specific language of the power of attorney document. The document can be prepared so that the powers begin as soon as the document is signed, or it can be prepared so that the powers "spring" into effect in the future when a particular event occurs (for example, when the principal is no longer competent—perhaps due to a physical or mental illness). Defining exactly when a "springing" power of attorney is to become effective oftentimes can be very difficult.

When do they then end? Powers of the attorney-in-fact end whenever the principal revokes (cancels) the power of attorney. Unless the power of attorney is a durable power of attorney, it ends by operation of law upon the happening of an event such as your becoming incapacitated. If the power of attorney document does contain certain language extending it beyond this event (thus making it durable), the powers of the attorney-in-fact will continue, but, according to the law, the powers will end when the principal dies. At such time either the will takes over or the trust document controls.

There are several common uses for a power of attorney. As parents get older, they sometimes need help paying their bills and handling other banking matters even though they are not incapacitated or incompetent. A parent can designate their child as attorney-in-fact rather than adding the child as an owner of a bank account. In addition, someone who plans to take an extended trip outside the country or who is recuperating from a long illness may wish to name a friend or relative as attorney-in-fact to pay bills or address property concerns.

o   Special/Limited

The power of attorney can be "special" or "limited," giving the attorney-in-fact only very limited powers (such as the power to sell the principal's vehicle). Many persons use these limited POAs to cover child care when leaving a child with someone while the parents are away. Or, if a spouse is transferred, each gives the other a POA to allow the sale of a residence at one location while the other buys a residence at the new location.

o   General

The power of attorney can be "general," giving the attorney-in-fact all of the powers that the principal would have if personally present. These are generally used between spouses and parents and children. They basically give full authority to the attorney-in-fact to do anything you could do if you are present. They can sell a house, close bank accounts, buy automobiles and so on. Therefore giving such power to another should be done with caution.

o   Durable

The power of attorney can be durable meaning it will survive a persons mental incapacity or incompetence, disability, disappearance and confinement. A typical provision appearing in such documents resembles the following:

> *"This is a durable power of attorney. The rights, powers, and authority of my attorney-in-fact shall be in full force and effect until my death. This power of attorney shall not terminate on my subsequent disability or incapacity.*
>
> *As used herein, "disability" or "incapacity" shall mean that my ability to receive and evaluate information effectively or to communicate decisions, or both, is impaired to such an extent that I lack the capacity to manage my financial resources as determined by the certification of at least one licensed physician, and shall include by inability to take actions due to voluntary or involuntary detention or disappearance, as determined by affidavit of my attorney-in-fact or another with knowledge regarding the same. I hereby waive any physician-client privilege for this limited purpose and authorize the disclosure or such certification by the physician to my attorney-in-fact for use by that person as necessary hereunder."*

CHAPTER 4

Exactly, what are advance directives? Advance directives are written documents, signed by you, that communicate your health care wishes to doctors and other health care professionals when you cannot speak for yourself. There are several types of legal forms that can be used to communicate your health care wishes. These advance directives include a living will, a durable health care power of attorney, a durable power of attorney for financial affairs and a form for making an anatomical gift (organ and tissue donation form). Another type of advance directive, called a do not resuscitate (DNR) Order, is completed by a doctor or other appropriate health care professional for use in limited situations.

There are many different types of advanced directives. Remember, each type serves a different purpose; so, depending upon your situation, you may wish to have more than one. For example, a living will tells health care professionals the kind of care you would want if you could not make your wishes known and you were terminally ill or permanently unconscious. A health care power of attorney allows you to name someone to make health care decisions for you if you become unable to do so. Through an organ and tissue donation form, you can name an individual or an organization to receive the gift of organs or tissues to be used for transplantation, therapy, research, education or advancement of medical or dental science upon your death. A DNR order is a physician order written in your medical records that says cardiopulmonary resuscitation or CPR is not to be administered to you.

Advance directives are not new. The living will declaration and health care power of attorney are not new, but the law changes periodically. It is therefore advisable to have these documents reviewed regularly.

- Living Wills

A living will declaration is a legal document that states your wishes concerning the use of life-sustaining treatment if you should become terminally ill or permanently unconscious. A living will:
  ❖ becomes effective only when you cannot communicate your wishes and are permanently unconscious or terminally ill;
  ❖ spells out whether or not you want life-support technology used to prolong your dying;
  ❖ authorizes doctors to follow your instructions about the medical treatment you want under these conditions;
  ❖ can be changed or revoked by you (and only you) at any time;

❖ will be followed for a pregnant woman only if certain conditions apply; and

❖ specifies under what conditions you would want artificial feeding and fluids to be withheld.

Even if your living will says you don't want to be hooked up to life-support equipment, you can still get pain medication. A living will only affects care that artificially or technologically postpones death. It does not affect care that eases pain such as oxygen, pain medication, spoon-feeding, and being turned over in bed.

One major concern is who should make the decision that you are in a permanently unconscious or terminally ill state of health. If you've indicated that you don't want your dying to be artificially prolonged, two doctors who have examined you must agree that you are beyond any medical help and that you will not recover. Your physicians will attempt to contact the person(s) named in your living will or your durable power of attorney for health care, and your family.

Remember, living wills are not just for the sick or elderly. Even if you are in perfect health and only age 23, it is a good idea to not only have a living will but other advance health care documents as well. Accidents and illness know no age boundaries. The younger you are the more likely loved ones will want to prolong your life even though that would not be your choice given the circumstances. At age 25, Nancy Cruzan was thrown from a car and went into an irreversible coma. Because she didn't have a living will or durable power of attorney, her family struggled in the courts, including the U.S. Supreme Court, for seven years before life-support machines could be turned off.

Before doctors stop life-support treatments, your family likely would be informed. Although doctors do not need your family's permission to follow the instructions provided through your living will, they must make reasonable efforts to notify a person named in your living will, or a family member, before following your instructions to withdraw life-support. If the notified person feels your living will isn't being properly followed, or isn't legally valid, an immediate hearing can be scheduled in probate court to determine if there are legal grounds not to follow your instructions. By law, however, no one can change or overrule your living will if it was freely and correctly executed. Like life support, feeding and fluids can be withheld if you wish.

If you are in a terminal condition, no special instructions are needed to allow the withholding of nutrition and hydration unless such measures are to provide comfort or relieve your pain. However, if you want to allow your doctor to withhold artificial nutrition/hydration if you are permanently unconscious, your document must expressly state this.

After you complete the forms required by your state, make several copies. Give one to a trusted member of your family. Keep another with your personal papers.

Leave copies with your physician and your lawyer, and, perhaps, your clergy person. If you are admitted to a hospital or nursing home, make a copy available to the health care providers and ask that a copy be placed in your medical chart.

Suppose you want all treatments to continue if you become critically ill. If there is no evidence that you do not want CPR or other life sustaining treatment, your health care providers will use all reasonable means to keep you alive. However, if you wish to spell out your wishes in this regard, you cannot use the standard form. You should talk with an attorney and your physician about the effect of such a decision.

- Durable Health Care Power of Attorney

A durable health care power of attorney is a legal document that authorizes another person to make health care decisions for you if you are unable to make informed health care decisions for yourself. A health care power of attorney:

- ❖ names an individual you trust to make a wide variety of health care decisions for you at any time you cannot do so for yourself, whether or not your condition is terminal;
- ❖ becomes effective only when you cannot make your own decisions regarding treatment;
- ❖ requires the person you appoint to make decisions that are consistent with your wishes; and

❖ will not overrule a living will in the event you have both documents.

The question arises as to why you need both a living will as well as a health care power of attorney. The reason is that these documents address different aspects of your medical care. A living will gives your instructions directly to your doctor. The living will applies only when you cannot communicate your wishes, you are in a terminal condition, or you are in a permanently unconscious state.

A durable health care power of attorney covers a wide range of health care decisions - such as approving surgery or changing doctors after an accident - that do not require a patient to be dying. Often a spouse or relative is selected to act on your behalf when you cannot, because such a person knows you well enough to know what you would want done. The person selected must know you well enough to be able to carry out all of your end-of-life care wishes.

If you have a durable health care power of attorney, you may save your family or friends the time and trouble of having to go to court to be appointed your legal guardian in order to make health care decisions on your behalf. Guardianship is a process that takes time, can be costly, and makes your health care status a public, rather than a private, matter.

Thus if you or someone is in a nursing home and if you or that person executed a durable power of attorney for health care, that attorney-in-fact could act on your behalf in every area affecting treatment, but not until you are no longer able to make those decisions on your own behalf. A durable power of attorney for health care covers not just life-sustaining treatment, but all aspects of medical treatment whenever the patient is unable to express their own wishes. A regular power of attorney over a relative's business affairs doesn't apply to medical situations. You need a durable power of attorney for health care. The designated person does not need to be a member of the patient's family. You may appoint any adult you wish as long as it isn't your doctor or the administrator of a health care facility in which you are being treated.

Many people find themselves with multiple residences during the year – winters in Florida and summers up North. This fact will not affect the provisions in your health care power of attorney and your living will, since each state honors the wishes expressed in your health care power of attorney and living will to the extent that state's law allows. It is advisable, therefore, to have your documents reviewed to determine if these state's laws differ in any material manner.

- Anatomical Gifts

Approximately 25,500 organ transplants were performed in the United States in 2003; more than 6,800 of those were from living donors. Another 950,000 Americans receive donor tissue each year through reconstructive, restorative and cosmetic surgeries. Nevertheless, in November 2004, more than 87,000 individuals were waiting for life-saving organ transplants. To help meet the need for organ and tissue donors, the many state legislatures have passed several pieces of legislation to encourage donation. The legislation is intended to increase the dissemination of information about organ and tissue donation, make it easy for persons to become donors, and provide workplace incentives for employees who serve as living donors.

Organs that can be donated include the heart, lungs, liver, kidneys, pancreas and small intestine. Tissues that can be donated include skin, bone, ligaments, tendons, fascia, veins, heart valves and corneas. If you wish to donate your entire body, you must contact the medical school of your choice to declare your intent.

Depending on the state you are in, there are requirements for registration as a donor. In Ohio, for example, Ohio established the Ohio Donor Registry in July 2002. The registry's database is maintained by the Ohio Bureau of Motor Vehicles (BMV), and allows only organ, tissue and eye procurement organizations access 24 hours a day, seven days a week. Your registration as a donor is an "advance directive" for your organs, tissues and/ or eyes, if usable, to be recovered upon your death. You can declare your wish to become a donor when renewing your driver's license or state identification card, or by completing the Donor Registry Enrollment Form available online at "www.ohiobmv.com". In addition to registering your intent, you should discuss your wishes with your family. An individual under 18 years of age who wishes to become a donor must have the consent of a parent or guardian.

Many states, like Ohio, allow designation for any intended use of an anatomical gift. These uses cover transplantation, therapy, research, education, or advancement of medical or dental science. All of these possible uses are listed on the Ohio Donor Registry Enrollment Form. If any of these possible uses is not acceptable to you, you should mark through the use or uses to which you object.

Life-saving organs allocated by the United Network for Organ Sharing (UNOS) maintains a national, computerized list of more than 87,000 patients awaiting kidney, heart, lung, liver, intestine, and pancreas transplants. Donors are matched against the list of recipients before an organ is offered for transplantation. Specific information about a donor is entered into the UNOS computer by an organ procurement organization. The computer first rules out potential recipients who are not compatible for blood type and body size. The computer then calculates a rank order for each remaining patient on the list. A patient's priority point score is determined by a number of variables including medical urgency, time waiting, and the degree of match with the donor. The UNOS computer does not consider race, income, or social status when determining potential recipients. The offer for the available organ is then made by the organ procurement organization to the identified patient's transplant center.

If you have a living will or durable health care power of attorney executed in Ohio before December 15, 2004, and you want to include an anatomical gift, you may want to have these documents redrawn. Legislation that became effective on September 16, 2004 permits you to state within your living will, your intent to donate an anatomical gift upon your death. According to Ohio law, living will forms are now required to include these provisions. Other states may have similar requirements.

To make sure your Ohio anatomical gift intentions are carried out in a timely manner, you should also complete and send to the BMV a Donor Registry Enrollment Form. An Enrollment Form is provided at the end of the living will form; you can detach it and send it directly to the BMV. You should make a copy of this form before you send it to the BMV and keep this copy with your living will. In the current Ohio forms, there is also a place to check to indicate you do not wish to become a donor.

In summary, remember, in Ohio you can still use your old living will, and the wishes you've expressed in that living will should still be honored. However, if you intend to create a living will after December 15, 2004, and you live in Ohio, your document should state your preference about making an anatomical gift using the specific language the law requires. Also, remember that if you do want to make such a gift, you should do more than state your wishes in your living will document. You should also complete the Donor

Registry Enrollment Form and send it to the Bureau of Motor Vehicles so your name can be added to Ohio's official donor registry.

- Mental Health Declarations

Before a law allowing for a mental health declaration goes into effect, the only document that could be used to name someone to make health decisions for another person was the durable power of attorney (DPOA). The DPOA addresses both physical and mental health issues, and still is sufficient in many states.

Unlike some other health care issues, however, mental health issues can be more complex and their specific treatments (e.g., medication therapies) generally are not addressed in a DPOA. If you have a mental illness or have been diagnosed with a mental illness in the past, and you already have a DPOA, you also may wish to have a mental health declaration to address issues that might arise and are not specifically covered by your health care DPOA and your state of residence allows such a declaration. The mental health declaration lets health care professionals know your own preferences regarding mental health treatment. It also allows the person you have named in the declaration (your "proxy") to advocate for your stated choices and make other decisions in your best interest if you have not stated any preferences.

A mental health declaration generally allows you to name an individual you know and trust to make decisions about your mental health treatment when you are unable to make them yourself; specifies when and how the declaration is used; specifically outlines the duties and rights of the person you designated to make your mental health decisions when you cannot while protecting that person from liability; provides that your mental health declaration designee (proxy) cannot be overridden by a designee of any other durable health care power of attorney regarding decisions about your mental health; specifies that, if you have lost your capacity to make informed decisions about your mental health treatment, you will not be able to revoke or cancel the mental health declaration; and stipulates that, if you have a living will, the living will overrides the mental health declaration.

Those who would benefit from having such a document include people who have been diagnosed with mental illness or people who think they might need mental health treatment at some point (for example, those of advanced age or those who have a progressive illness that is likely to involve mental health issues).

Before you make any decisions to see if you need a mental health declaration, you would be wise to contact your lawyer to discuss the options available. Your lawyer also can help you complete the necessary form for a mental health declaration. You should also discuss your treatment preferences with any mental health professional who may be providing services to you.

In Ohio, the Ohio General Assembly passed legislation creating a Declaration of Mental Health Treatment, a document that allows individuals to state their own preferences regarding mental health treatment and to appoint a person to make mental health care decisions for them when they are unable to do so themselves.

Specifically, Ohio's mental health declaration:
- ❖ allows you to name an individual you know and trust to make decisions about your mental health treatment when you are unable to make them yourself;
- ❖ specifies when and how the declaration is used;
- ❖ specifically outlines the duties and rights of the person you designated to make your mental health decisions when you cannot and protects that person from liability;
- ❖ provides that your mental health declaration designee (proxy) cannot be overridden by the designee of any other durable health care power of attorney regarding decisions about your mental health;
- ❖ specifies that, if you have lost your capacity to make informed decisions about your mental health treatment, you will not be able to revoke or cancel the mental health declaration;
- ❖ stipulates that the living will overrides the mental health declaration.

Those who would benefit from having such a document include people who have been diagnosed with mental illness or people who think they might need mental health treatment at some point (for example, those of advanced age or those who have a progressive illness that is likely to involve mental health issues). If you feel it desirable to have a mental health declaration you should consult a professional concerning both the legal requirements and treatment provisions.

- Guardianships

We have talked about advance care planning as being a type of estate and life planning that focuses on planning for when a person becomes ill, disabled, incompetent or incapacitated. The advance care documents we discussed allow you to state your own wishes about medical treatment and to privately appoint someone to act as your agent in financial or health care matters if and when you cannot make your wishes known. The most common and simplest advance care planning documents were the durable power of attorney for financial matters, durable power of attorney for health care, living will and trusts.

Guardianships differ from these other advance care documents because they are court created and generally result because there was no advance care planning. The terms are between the court and the guardian they appoint. Further guardianships are more expensive because they involve court hearings, bonding, court supervision and may be involuntarily created upon a showing that the person cannot take care of themselves. The probate court creates and oversees a guardianship and entrusts the guardian with the care of another (the "ward"). This relationship includes a financial obligation to the ward (a "fiduciary" relationship). On the other side, the drafting and execution of a power of attorney is a private matter with no court involvement. A power of attorney can allow the attorney-in-fact named in the document to make financial and/or health care decisions for the "principal." The principal downsides are the lack of oversight and ability for the attorney-in-fact to use the funds for other matters. Care must to taken to ensure complete trust in the appointee.

The process to appoint a guardian may be necessary if there is no other alternative. The process can take time. First, a probate court must find that the intended "ward" is incompetent. You, as the proposed guardian, must give the court a medical doctor's expert evaluation that states the ward is incompetent. Then, the court must find that the ward needs a guardian because there is no less restrictive alternative. If there is such an alternative, the probate court will deny the guardianship application. For example, the court may find that your father's care can be managed through one or more powers of attorney (financial and/or health care) rather than through a guardianship. Finally, the probate court will determine whether you are suitable to serve as guardian. Family members generally are the preferred guardians.

There may be a limited need for a guardianship. For instance, if all financial matters are taken care of through a trust, only health care issues may need managing. In those circumstances a probate court can appoint a "guardian of the person," which is different from a "guardian of the estate" or "conservator". The latter has authority over the ward's assets and finances while the former has control over the person and their care. Although a court usually appoints a guardian of both the person and the estate, any person can apply to be guardian of just one or the other. As guardian of the person only, you will not have control over another's finances and will not need to post a bond or report on their assets to the court.

Likewise, if there is no living will, oftentimes family members ask the probate court to appoint a guardian of the person for end-of-life decisions. Once appointed, a guardian may agree or refuse to authorize medical care as being in the ward's best interest without a probate court order unless interested parties object or the probate court orders otherwise. Your family should check to see if your state has a "Family Consent Statute" which generally will provide a way for the family of a terminally ill or permanently unconscious patient to consent to withhold life-sustaining treatment. A living will can prove much less expensive and complex to implement.

Complications can arise where you have given someone a power of attorney, have executed other health care documents such as a living will and durable power of attorney for health care and another family member seeks authority from a probate court to be appointed as a guardian. What documents control? Simply put, the appointment of a guardian by the court does not automatically revoke a validly executed power of attorney or other advance care document. However, the law may allow a guardian to revoke all or any part of the power and authority of any attorney-in-fact and other health care document. Therefore, someone acting under the original power of attorney would have continuing authority to act on one's behalf until the guardian revokes the powers of attorney or other documents. If you anticipate such a problem, it is vitally necessary for all parties to appear before the probate court before it appoints a guardian to settle these issues and avoid possible conflict with your wishes.

In conclusion, a guardianship is an excellent way to ensure that a person's personal needs are met and that the ward's assets are protected. The fact that the court monitors the administration of the guardianship helps ensure that matters are handled in an efficient and orderly manner. Nonetheless, because guardianships are matters of public record, you may wish to avoid the need for one. Likewise, you may wish to avoid paying a guardian and an attorney. Accordingly, you should consider one of two generally accepted guardianship alternatives: (1) a living trust, and (2) durable power of attorney.

Remember from our previous discussion, if you set up a revocable living trust, whomever you name as the trustee of that trust will be able to manage any trust-owned assets. Accordingly, if you were to transfer (or fund) your own trusts during your lifetime, the trust assets may be used for your benefit without the need of court supervision. This is a highly desirable feature especially if, for instance, your spouse or another close family member is named as successor trustee. In such a case, the trust assets can be used to meet your needs until the assets are exhausted.

Likewise, you may wish to use powers of attorney to ensure that your assets and health care are managed. Through a health care power of attorney, you will name an agent to make health care decisions on your behalf, and without court supervision, if you become incapacitated.

Through a durable general power of attorney, you can name an attorney-in-fact to handle legal and financial affairs on your behalf both before and after you become incapacitated. This is a useful feature, especially for those who do not have "funded living trusts". The attorney-in-fact will see that your legal and financial needs are met, but will not have a duty to account to the court. If you decide a living trust is useful, you should also have a durable health care power of attorney and a financial power of attorney to address what is not covered through the living trust.

- Do Not Resuscitate Orders (DNR)

DNR stands for "do not resuscitate." A person who does not wish to have cardiopulmonary resuscitation (CPR) performed may make this wish known through a doctor's order called a DNR order. A DNR order addresses the various methods used to revive people whose hearts have stopped functioning or who have stopped breathing. Examples of these treatments include chest compressions, electric heart shock, artificial breathing tubes, and special drugs. Many states have what are called DNR Comfort Care Protocols. In Ohio, the Ohio Department of Health has established two standardized DNR order forms. When completed by a physician (or certified nurse practitioner or clinical nurse specialist, as appropriate), these standardized DNR orders allow patients to choose the extent of the treatment they wish to receive at the end of life. A patient with a "DNR Comfort Care-Arrest Order" will receive all the appropriate medical treatment, including resuscitation, until the patient has a cardiac or pulmonary arrest, at which point only comfort care will be provided. By requesting the broader "DNR Comfort Care Order," a patient may reject other life-sustaining measures such as drugs to correct abnormal heart rhythms. With this order, only comfort care would be provided at a point even before the heart or breathing stops. Your doctor can explain the differences in DNR orders.

You may authorize a "Do Not Resuscitate (DNR)" order through your living will. This living will DNR is useful for conveying your wishes to family members and medical staff; however, it will not be activated unless two doctors have agreed that you are either terminally ill or permanently unconscious, and your personal doctor has agreed that you can no longer express your wishes regarding health care.

Your physician may write a DNR order for you in your medical record or prepare a DNR order in advance on a state's DNR order form. If you do not wish to receive CPR, you should inform your physician, family members, and the person you've chosen to be the attorney-in-fact for your health care power of attorney.

Why consider a DNR? Although in some cases it does save lives, CPR (cardiopulmonary resuscitation) frequently is not successful or does not benefit those who receive it, especially for elderly people or those with serious medical conditions. Resuscitation can involve such things as drugs, forcefully pressing on the chest, giving electric shocks to restart the heart or placing a tube down the nose or throat to provide artificial breathing. For more information about the pros and cons of CPR and whether it is right for you, talk with your doctor.

But, if you do want to receive CPR when it is medically appropriate, you do not have to do anything. Emergency squads and other health care providers must provide CPR whenever medically appropriate. However, if you do not want CPR, you always have the right to refuse it (or any other medical treatment), but most likely you will not be able to state your wishes when an emergency happens. Therefore, if you do not want CPR, you should again discuss your wishes with your doctor about whether it would be appropriate for you to have a DNR order. While your doctor is not required to use a standard form, its use will be easily recognized by paramedics and other health care workers.

States have adopted DNR laws for a variety of purposes similar to the implementation of other life saving decisions regarding the use of life support equipment and administering fluids and nourishment. But only doctors can issue "do not resuscitation orders". And many times heart failure occurs outside the hospital where emergency medical professionals (EMP) are generally involved. Without a DNR order on file, these EMPs must administer CPR and other heart responses or face liability. The primary purpose of the DNR laws is to help people communicate their wishes about resuscitation to medical personnel outside a hospital or nursing home setting. It allows emergency medical workers to honor patients' physician-written DNR orders even if they are at home rather than in the hospital when the heart or breathing stops. This law protects emergency squads and other health care providers from liability if they follow their patients' DNR orders outside a hospital or nursing home setting.

If you are a patient in a hospital or nursing home, the DNR order should be in your medical chart. You or your family also should notify the medical staff that you have such an order any time you are admitted to a facility or are transferred from one facility to another. If, on the other hand, you are receiving care at home, you should request your doctor issue you a DNR and then tell your family and caregivers where to find your DNR order. You also may want to talk with your doctor about getting DNR identification such as a wallet card or bracelet that tells medical personnel you have a DNR order. Then medical emergency personnel will be ware of your wishes.

Remember, if you are unable to express your wishes, other people such as your legal guardian or a person you named in a durable health care power of attorney may speak for you. You should make sure these people know your desires about CPR. If your doctor writes a DNR order at your request, your family cannot override it. If you change your mind, you always have the right to request CPR. If you do change your mind, you should talk with your doctor right away about revoking your DNR order. You also should tell your family and caregivers about your decision, mark "cancelled" on the actual DNR order, and destroy any DNR wallet cards or other identification items you may have.

In states like Ohio, the standard living will declaration form can specifically direct your physician to write a DNR order for you if two doctors have agreed that you are either terminally ill or permanently unconscious. Your attorney-in-fact under your durable power of attorney for health care can then request the doctor write a DNR and place it in your medical records.

- HIPAA

Have you ever called the doctor on behalf of your spouse only to be told no one can speak to you? Likewise, has someone asked you to talk with Social Security or a health care insurance company for them and again you were told no one will speak to you? You check into a hospital and nobody can contact you because they cannot get the hospital to tell them you are even admitted. Have you noticed when going to the pharmacy that they have built cubicles or require you to remain at a distance from the counter when another customer is there? Welcome to the world created by the Federal Health Insurance Portability and Accountability Act or HIPAA for short.

The law was further implemented by rule change in April 2003 to better protect a patient's information and to provide more control over the patient's records. The penalties for violating the Act are significant. Organizations can be fined up to $25,000 if they do not adequately protect the information or refuse to give you your records when requested; individuals can face criminal charges with penalties up to ten (10) years in prison and fines up to $250,000.00 if they sell, transfer or use the information improperly. The law extends beyond hospitals and medical doctors' offices. It extends to government agencies such as Medicare and Social Security, health insurance companies, paramedics, firefighters, dentists, nurses, and pharmacies; even your clergy has been ensnared by overly cautious federal rule interpretations when they try to obtain a list of their parishioners from a hospital.

Because of these penalties, many of the covered people are very cautious to a fault. The US Department of Health and Human Services enforces the law. Since 2003, over 14,000 complaints have been filed. Thus, be sure when you check into a hospital or visit a doctor's office to request them to annotate your files as to whom you want to allow access to your files and information. Be sure you give copies of your Durable Health Care Power of Attorney or other authorization documents to your medical providers and insurance companies in order to ensure that your information can get to the right people when you need it most. Ask each what procedures they have in-place to allow you to name those to whom you want to give access, especially at times when you cannot.

While the previous chapters dealt with issues regarding your real property, material possessions, your health and your lineal and marital family, we must consider that other member of your family, the one the law considers property – your pets. In Chapter 5 we will explore the issues surrounding taking care of your pets after you cannot, and for their disposal after their death.

Chapter 5

- Pets, in general

Pets are often considered family members, but what happens to them when their owners become disabled or die? To plan for the proper care and transfer of ownership of pets, owners can use traditional estate planning methods and documents to cover many of these issues.

Under many state laws, including Ohio, pets are considered personal property and thus your pets will be distributed as part of your estate. If you have a valid will that makes a specific gift of your pets, those gifts will pass to the individual you selected to care for these pets. If you have not specifically given away your pets, the animals will become part of your residuary estate. The residuary is what is left of your estate after all claims, debts and gifts have been settled, and will pass to individuals you named as beneficiaries of your residuary estate.

o   Care and Maintenance

As a practical matter, upon your death, your executor and beneficiaries of your estate will need to find a home for the pets if the named beneficiaries are not willing or able to care for the pets. If you die without a will (intestate), the animals will pass to your heirs as specified by a state's statute of descent and distribution. Thus, whoever finally will be chosen to receive your pets will vary depending on your personal situation. To make sure your pets will be cared for by someone you choose, it is a good idea to make a will that names a beneficiary who is willing and able to care for your pets.

Under the law, animals cannot own property. This means you cannot leave your estate to a pet. You must leave it to somebody to use for the care and maintenance of that pet. You may give the property or money to an individual, either through a will or through a lifetime gift, and instruct that individual to use the funds for your pet's care. It is significant to know that under the law the individual you choose will own the property or money and there is little that could be done if the individual decides not carry out your wishes. Therefore, you should be very careful when selecting someone to receive property or money for the care of your pets.

Alternatively, you may create a trust to achieve greater certainty or specifically add to a power of attorney, provisions covering the care of pets. Under a power of attorney, you will direct the attorney-in-fact to expend funds for the care and maintenance of the pets during such time as you cannot. Such powers of attorney will end upon your death, so thought must be given to the use of a trust.

Trusts are more complicated. Unlike some states, Ohio law does not recognize pet trusts that name an animal as the trust beneficiary. However, you can create a trust naming an individual as a beneficiary to become your pets' caretaker or owner with instructions to the trustee to provide funds for the care of the animals. If you want to revise an existing trust or are considering creating a trust to care for your animals in case you die or become incapacitated, you should discuss the benefits and limitations of this approach with a lawyer

You also may want to make provisions for the short-term care of your pets in case of an emergency wherein you are injured or incapacitated. Many animals can suffer health consequences in a matter of hours if they do not receive proper care. Consider carrying a pet identification card that indicates you own animals, explains the special care they need, and provides a contact person. In case you are injured or incapacitated, emergency personnel would be able to notify a person who would take immediate action to care for your pets. In these situations, a power of attorney for a limited purpose can work well as it can give an individual authority to seek veterinary services in your name and absence.

o   Perpetual Care

Perpetual care has two meanings: (1) to provide continued care and a home for your pet during its life, but following your death, and (2) to provide cremation or burial and care for your pet after it dies. With regard to the first, there are now organizations such as public veterinary schools that provide a way to ensure the care of your pet after you die. Through your making a specific charitable bequest to the school through your will or by a pre-arranged agreement, a veterinary school will take over the care of those pets. One such school is at the University of Minnesota:

www.cvm.umn.edu/img/assets/14022/Perpetual_Care_
Brochure.pdf

Another such facility is at the University of Kansas:

www.vet.ksu.edu/depts/development/perpet/program

With regard to the second meaning, you can run into some of the same issues with pet cemeteries that you run into with regular cemeteries. You should exercise the same vigilance in arranging for perpetual care after your pet dies that you do for yourself. If pre-paid arrangements were made, be sure to include that information with your other memorial and funeral information. Be sure to mention the same in any trust and will documents. While such arrangements are not enforceable, the fact that they are pre-paid will help facilitate your wishes.

CHAPTER 6

Suppose you find yourself appointed as a fiduciary, or you may wonder what a fiduciary actually does before you appoint or hire one. There are many types of fiduciaries we mentioned in this book:

- ❖ Executors or Administrators of a Will;
- ❖ Trustees of a Living or Testamentary Trust;
- ❖ Attorneys-in-Fact under a Power of Attorney;
- ❖ Guardians of a Person and Estate; and
- ❖ Attorneys.

What is a fiduciary and what are they required to do? Principally, a fiduciary is a person who is entrusted with another's person, property and money. The fiduciary is then responsible for the care of a person or pet, the management of any property and money placed under the appointing document. The fiduciary is personally liable for the mismanagement of that obligation, both criminally (such as embezzlement) and civilly (for negligence). Generally the person bestowing the appointment on another will require a bond or surety to cover any misfeasance, nonfeasance or malfeasance. Court appointed fiduciaries are normally required to be bonded. But many times, where the fiduciary is a family member, the person appointing a fiduciary waives the bond in the appointing document to save the estate the cost. While many times this procedure has little risk (when the fiduciary and the beneficiary are one and the same), at other times it can be highly risky (when a person appoints their neighbor as an attorney-in-fact).

- Executors and Administrators Under a Will

The only difference between an executor and administrator is whether the deceased died with or without a will. A person appoints an executor under will, while a court appoints an administrator where a person dies without a will. In either case, the fiduciary performs the same duties. An executor/administrator will collect assets of the deceased not otherwise disposed of by a will substitute. The executor/administrator will pay valid outstanding debts and expenses of the estate with probate assets. The executor/ administrator will settle or litigate claims against the estate by creditors, heirs and others, file required papers with the court and others to include at a minimum – a request for appointment, inventory, motions to transfer certain property such as automobiles and realty, accounts, tax returns, close-outs and discharge. The executor/ administrator will make final distributions of probate property. The executor/administrator will turn over assets to any guardians appointed by the court or by the will. An executor or administrator is entitled to be paid for their services, although many times since they are also one of the beneficiaries, such fees are waived. They may hire others – attorneys, accountants and appraisers, for example – to assist in the administration of the estate.

- Trustees/Conservators

A trustee is the person appointed under a trust agreement to administer the terms of the trust. Trust agreements deal with management of the property placed in the trust to fund that trust. Like executors and administrators, trustees must pay due expenses and debts of the trust. They may have to file tax returns. They must control the capital and income of the trust with care and consistent with the terms of the trust. They must pay out sums to the beneficiaries according to the terms of the trust. They must settle or litigate claims against the trust. They may hire others – attorneys, accountants and appraisers, for example – to assist in the administration of the trust.

A conservator may be appointed by the court to accomplish the same functions as a trustee where a person is a minor or otherwise needs a guardian for an estate. In the case of a conservator, as an officer of the court, they report periodically to the court. The court supervises the administration of the estate placed under the conservator's responsibility and the conservator's authority extends only to that given by the court. A trustee may or may not have to report to the court depending on the appointing document.

- Attorneys-in-Fact

Attorneys-in-fact are appointed specifically in the power of attorney and have only that authority given to them by the document. We mentioned earlier that such powers are limited, general and durable. They can be given to allow management of certain assets (pay bills of a parent), accomplish certain functions (register an automobile for another) or care for certain people (make financial health decisions for minors). The attorney-in-fact is personably responsible for the performance of the duties given and must answer for any malfeasance, misfeasance or nonfeasance. A payment and performance bond is highly recommended unless you have extreme confidence in the attorney-in-fact to manage the assets or take care of the person.

- Guardians

Guardians are appointed under a will or by a court to manage the care and maintenance of another person, generally a minor or someone who is incompetent or can not otherwise take care of themselves. They are typically referred to as "guardians of the person" who manage the personal care decisions of the ward, or "guardians of the estate or conservator" who control the assets of the ward. If the guardian does not have control over the ward's assets, they may have to seek any funds they need from the conservator or "guardian of the estate" of the ward. Regardless, guardians are personally liable to their wards for any malfeasance, misfeasance or nonfeasance. Guardians make the decisions for those individuals that they believe are in their wards best interests.

- Attorneys

Attorneys hold positions as a fiduciary because of the unique position they play in the process. They represent clients – whether they are executors, administrators, attorneys-in-fact, guardians or conservators – and make decisions for them. They oftentimes hold monies on behalf of the client. Since attorneys must be licensed, they are under a code of professional responsibility and can lose their license if found guilty of malpractice or other improper practices. Likewise, other professionals such as accountants are equally responsible to their respective licensing agencies and codes of responsibility. Attorneys give legal advice, represent clients and prepare the legal documents needed by other fiduciaries and persons necessary to provide for estate and health care planning, administration and prosecution.

Appendix A:
Sample Form

Memorial and Burial & Other Wishes

of

_____

This document is intended to assist my family and friends during any last illness and at the time of my death. It is divided into three areas: 1. Information concerning my last illness, 2. Memorial/ Burial preferences, and 3. perpetual care for my pets. I request this document be given to that person responsible for arranging for my funeral and burial/ cremation and any beneficiary overseeing the care of my pets.

I understand that no one is legally obligated to comply with my desires concerning memorial matters stated herein. However, I would like for them to comply with these wishes, so long as doing so does not create an undue burden or financial hardship.

I have copies of estate planning documents (such as wills and trusts) and advance health care directives (such as a living will or health care power of attorney) attached to this document. Nothing in this document amends or changes the terms of those legal instruments. Any failure, on my part, to mention all of those documents or to identify any of them properly shall not be construed as expressing any intent on my part to amend or revoke any instrument.

Information Concerning My Last Illness

1. Advance Care Documents:

I have signed the following instruments concerning my treatment during any final illness where I am unable to communicate my own health care preferences:

2. Organ Donation:

I have signed the following document(s) concerning donation of my organs:

Memorial Preferences

1. Notification:

Please notify _____ at the time of my death.

2. Funeral Home/Director:

Arrangements (have/have not) been made in advance for funeral services. Please contact _____ to complete my final arrangements.

3. Disposition of Remains:

I prefer that my remains be handled as follows:

4. Services:

Following are my wishes concerning holding various kinds of services:

a. Funeral -

b. Memorial Service -

c. Wake -

d. Visitation:

5. Flowers, Memorial Funds, Donations:

6. Pallbearers:
Please ask the following people to serve as my pallbearers:

If any of the persons named are unable to serve for any reason, I would like you to ask the following persons to serve as alternate pallbearers, in this order:

7. <u>Perpetual Care for Pets:</u>

Arrangements (have/have not) been made in advance for the care and maintenance of my pets. There are (#) _____ and their names/breed are:

_____

Please contact _____ for additional information. In the absence of such arrangements, please follow any provisions made in my will. I (have/have not) made arrangements for cemetery and disposition services of these pets. Please contact _____ to complete my pet's final arrangements. It is my desire that my pet be (cremated/buried) at _____ and that funds of my estate not to exceed $_____ be allocated for that purpose.

Name: _____
Dated: _____

Appendix B:
Sample Questionnaire

CONFIDENTIAL ESTATE PLANNING QUESTIONNAIRE/
MARRIED PERSON

Personal Information as of: _____ 20____

Your Name: _____

Your Spouse's Name: _____

Home Address: _____

_____

Home Phone: _____ e-mail address: _____

Date of Birth: You: _____ Your Spouse: _____

Social Security Numbers: You: _____

Your Spouse: _____

Your Employer: _____

Business Phone: _____ cell phone: _____

Position: _____

Your Spouse's Employer? _____

Business Phone: _____ cell phone: _____

Position: _____

90

Your Children and/or other dependents (please list all of them):
Name: _____
Age: _____
Address: _____

ESTATE INFORMATION

The following information helps develop your estate plan documents. You and your spouse may wish to complete this information separately. If you combine your answers, please indicate the differences between your and your spouse's answers.

I. NAMING OF PERSONAL REPRESENTATIVE/ EXECUTOR

A personal representative or executor is in charge of your estate matters upon your death. The basic responsibilities of the personal representative or executor are: to identify and account for all the assets of the deceased person; to pay the debts of the deceased person; to file any required tax returns; and, to distribute the assets of the estate as required by the Will (or as required by law, if there is no Will).

A. Who would you like to appoint as the personal representative of your estate (also known as the executor)?

B. Who would you appoint as an alternate personal representative should the person first named be unwilling or unable to serve?

II. NAMING OF TRUSTEE

A Trustee is in charge of any assets that you may leave in trust. The trustee is usually given broad grants of authority to deal with such assets.

A. Who would you designate as trustee of a trust you create (if any)?

B. If the trustee named above is unwilling or unable to serve as trustee, who would you appoint as successor trustee (you may want to designate a financial institution such as a bank as a successor trustee; the reason for this is that the bank will continue in existence indefinitely, whereas individuals who are named as trustees may predecease the termination date of the trust)?

III. GUARDIANS OF YOUR MINOR CHILD(REN)

A Guardian takes care of the "person" or "estate" of another individual. The Guardian has duties similar to a parent's duties to a minor child.

A. Who would you request as guardian of you minor children?

B. Who would you request as guardian of your minor children should the first named person(s) be unwilling or unable to serve?

IV. SPECIFIC OTHER INFORMATION

A. EXISTING WILLS OR TRUSTS.
   Do you have existing Wills or Trusts?

B. INHERITED PROPERTY.
   Have either of you received a substantial amount of property from an inheritance, a gift, or as a beneficiary of a trust?

C. FUTURE INHERITANCE.
   Do either of you anticipate any sizable inheritance or are you the beneficiary of an existing probate estate or trust? If so, please indicate the approximate value and nature of your share.

D. GIFTS.
   Have either of you made any gifts requiring a gift tax return (generally, present gifts in excess of $11,000 in value)? If so, please indicate the value and date of the gift(s).

E. JOINTLY OWNED PROPERTY, including POD, TOD, real and personal (tangible and intangible)
Do either of you own property jointly with a third party or do you own property which is payable on your death to another? If so, please describe.

F. LIFE INSURANCE/ANNUITIES.

(a) Do you have life insurance or annuity policies on your life? Please provide the face amount(s); type of insurance (term, whole life, etc.).

(b) Does a third party (individual or corporation) own life insurance on the life of either of you or do either of you own life insurance on the life of someone else? If so, please indicate the name of the owner, the cash value, and the face amount of the policy(ies).

(c) Do you plan on purchasing additional insurance in the near future?

G. MARITAL MATTERS.

(a) Have either of you been divorced? Do you have a copy of the decree?

(b) Do you have a written agreement regarding your marital relationship (for example, an ante-nuptial or pre-nuptial agreement)?

H. SPECIFIC BEQUESTS

Do you have any specific bequests of property you would like to make (for example, to charity or specific persons of specific dollar amounts)(Please list their names, addresses and relationships):

I. DISTRIBUTION OF PROPERTY
(The following assumes you prefer to distribute your estate to your children.

   (a) If you have minor children, you may want a trust to be created for their benefit. The terms of the trust can be varied, but typically property is held in trust until the minor children reach the age of 35 years. The property is held in a single trust for the benefit of all children until the point in time where all the children are at least age 21. After that date, the children are usually entitled to all the income from the trust and a trustee retains the principal. The trustee has the discretion to use the principal for the health, maintenance, welfare and education needs of the children during this time. When the child reaches the age of 25 years, one-third of the principal of the trust is distributed outright. When the child reaches the age of 30 years, an addition-al one-third of the trust principal is distributed outright. Upon the child reaching the age of 35 years, the remaining trust, principal and income, are distributed outright and the trust terminates.

   (b) If you have more than one child and one of your children predeceases the other child, would you prefer that the deceased child's share go to your other children, or would you rather see the deceased child's share go to such child's children, should he/she have any children (per stirpes)?

   (c) If the deceased child is not survived by children but is survived by a spouse, would you wish to see that surviving spouse take the deceased child's share or would you rather have that share transferred to your other surviving children?

J. FUNERAL ARRANGEMENTS
Are there any special funeral arrangements you would like to see made (typically, the surviving spouse is named to take care of such arrangements and another person is designated should

the surviving spouse be unable or unwilling to make such arrangements)?

K. SIZE OF ESTATE

The value of the estate's assets is needed to determine whether "Estate Taxes" will be due upon your death. For the most part, federal estate taxes are not usually a factor in estates of less than $650,000.00. However, you may want to consider more sophisticated estate planning if the value of your estate is at or near the sum of $500,000.00.

(a) Does your gross estate, including the face amount of life insurance policies on your life, and including the fair market value of all your other assets, less liabilities, exceed $650,000?

(b) Do you have a safe deposit box? _____
Location of box and key _____

(c) List all items and approximate value of your estate not listed elsewhere, i.e., automobiles, RVs, boats, vacation properties, time shares, household goods, jewelry (of value), antiques, stocks, bonds, CDs, etc.

Appendix C:

Sample Outline of a Living Trust: Do not copy or use without consultation with an attorney. Every person's situation is different.

LIVING TRUST

of

[Grantor]

[Parties to Trust Agreement.] THIS AGREEMENT is made , between [Grantor] of [County], [State], referred to as "Grantor," and [Trustee] of [Trustee's County], [Trustee's State], referred to as "Trustee."

[Introduction.] Grantor is creating a revocable trust for the purposes set forth in this Agreement. Grantor, therefore, is transferring to the Trustee the property listed in the attached schedule. The Trustee shall hold the property and any other property which the Trustee may acquire from Grantor or from other people, all of which is collectively referred to as the "trust," in trust, upon the following terms.

ARTICLE I

DISTRIBUTION OF TRUST PROPERTY

(A) [Distribution during life of Grantor.]

(B) [Distribution of specific bequests upon death of Grantor.]

(C) [Clause upon Grantor's death, to distribute all the rest of Grantor's tangible and intangible personal property not disposed of in Paragraph (B) of this Article I, or all of Grantor's tangible and intangible personal property if there are no specific bequests of personal property, to ... specific persons]

(D) [Residual clause upon Grantor's death, to divide the rest, residue and remainder of the principal and any undistributed net income of the trust (together with any other property to which the Trustee may be entitled by reason of Grantor's death and less any taxes, debts, expenses or other obligations payable by the Trustee as a result of Grantor's death) to named persons into specific trusts.]

    1. [Trust A. The first share (to be created only if Grantor's spouse, [Spouse], survives Grantor), called "Trust A," shall be in an amount equal to the value of all property to be divided into shares, reduced by the lesser of (i) the maximum amount that will avoid any federal estate tax being due in Grantor's estate, or (ii) the maximum amount that will avoid any state death tax being due in Grantor's estate, whichever of said two amounts is less.]

    2. [Trust B. The second share, called "Trust B," shall consist of that property which is not included in Trust A or, if Grantor's spouse does not survive Grantor, it shall consist of all the property.]

(E) The Trustee shall distribute Trust A as follows:

    1. While Grantor's spouse, [Spouse], is living, the Trustee:

(a) Shall pay to Grantor's spouse, any net income of the trust that Grantor's spouse may from time to time request in writing without limitation as to the amounts of or the reasons for such withdrawals of income. The Trustee shall accumulate the net income of the trust not so requested by Grantor's spouse and add it to the principal of the trust at such times as the Trustee shall determine.

(b) Shall pay to Grantor's spouse from the principal of Trust A, property or sums of money that Grantor's spouse, from time, requests in writing, without limitation as to the amounts of or the reasons for the withdrawals.

2. Upon the death of Grantor's spouse:

(a) The Trustee shall distribute the principal and undistributed net income of Trust A to, or in trust for, such persons or corporations or the estate of Grantor's spouse in those amounts or proportions designated by specific reference to this power in Grantor's spouse's last Will.

3. [Tax issues and how to handle them]

(a) During the lifetime of Grantor's spouse, the Trustee shall not, without the consent of Grantor's spouse, retain beyond a reasonable time any property which is unproductive or invest in unproductive property.

(b) No power or discretion granted to the Trustee by any other provision of this Agreement shall be exercised or exercisable by the Trustee, except to the extent and in the manner consistent with the allowance of the marital deduction, and any question pertaining to Trust A shall be resolved accordingly.

(F) The Trustee shall distribute Trust B as follows:

1. [While Grantor's spouse, [Spouse], is living, the Trustee shall pay to Grantor's spouse, not less often than quarter-annually, all the net income of Trust B.]

2. [Following the death of Grantor's spouse or following Grantor's death if Grantor's spouse does not survive Grantor, and until no living child of Grantor is under twenty-one years of age, the Trustee shall pay to Grantor's children and to the descendants of any deceased children from time to time part or all of the net income of the trust as the Trustee shall determine is advisable to provide for their support, medical care and education (including college and professional education)].

(a) [Each share created for a child of Grantor who is then living shall constitute a separate trust.]

(b) [Each share created for a deceased child of Grantor who has one or more descendants then living shall be distributed to the then living descendants of the deceased child, per stirpes.]

(G) [If, when any separate trust is ended, none of the intended beneficiaries of the trust is living, the Trustee shall distribute the property to whomever and in the same proportions as, Grantor's Personal Representative would have been required to distribute it had Grantor died intestate, unmarried, and a resident of the state of Ohio at such time and owning such property.]

ARTICLE II

ALTERNATE DISTRIBUTION PROVISIONS

Regardless of any contrary provisions:

(A) [If, when any separate trust is ended, any part of the principal of the trust is distributable to any person for whose benefit the Trustee shall then be holding any part of another share in trust, that part of the principal shall be added to and disposed of as a part of the other trust, under all the terms that pertain to it.]

(B) [Grantor may transfer, from time to time, certain tangible personal property to this trust by assignment, bill of sale or other written instrument delivered to the Trustee, the possession of which property Grantor shall retain in the individual capacity of Grantor.]

(C) [If, when any separate trust is ended, any part of the principal of the trust is distributable to a person who is under twenty-one years of age, the Trustee may, in the discretion of the Trustee, withhold distribution of the property and invest it and collect the income from it until the beneficiary attains twenty-one years of age.]

(D) [Grantor may transfer from time to time, certain real property to this trust by Deed recorded with the appropriate Office of Recorder of Deeds, the possession of which real property Grantor shall retain in the individual capacity of Grantor.] .

(E) [In the event Grantor and Grantor's spouse are divorced or their marriage is dissolved, any provisions in the trust in favor of Grantor's spouse shall be revoked and the trust shall be administered as though Grantor's divorced spouse had died at the time of the divorce or dissolution.]

ARTICLE III

SUPPLEMENTAL TRUST PROVISIONS

The provisions in this Agreement for the distribution of the trust shall be supplemented by the following:

(A)-(K) [Additional specified administrative powers to be give the trustee if desired]

ARTICLE IV

ADMINISTRATIVE POWERS OF TRUSTEE

In addition to the existing authority of the Trustee, and unless this Trust Agreement provides otherwise, the Trustee may:

(A)-(Q) [Additional powers to spell out regarding what trustee can do.]

ARTICLE V

TRUSTEE PROVISIONS

(A) The Trustee acknowledges receipt from Grantor of the property constituting the trust and accepts the trust upon the terms herein set forth.

(B) [Appointment of trustee.]

(C) Bonding Requirement.]

(D) Provisions regarding interpreting this Agreement.

1. Throughout this Trust Agreement the use of any gender shall be deemed to include all genders, and the use of the singular the plural, and vice versa. The terms "child" and "descendant" shall include an adopted person and such adopted person's descendants.

2. The captions of Articles and paragraphs appearing herein are for convenience of reference only and shall have no significance in the construction or interpretation of this Trust Agreement.

(E) [Trustee Voluntary Resignation Provision.]

(F) [Trustee Involuntary Resignation Provision.]

(G) [Requirement on inventories or accountings.]

(H) [Limitation on discretionary distributions]

(I) [The Trustee may employ such investment counsel, advisers, custodians, agents and assistants as the Trustee shall deem advisable and limitation of liability.]

ARTICLE VI
AMENDMENT OF TRUST AND
MISCELLANEOUS PROVISIONS

(A) [Powers to change trust by others}

(B) [Applications of powers]

(C) [Grantor's ability to amend trust]

(D) [Additional powers of grantor]

IN WITNESS WHEREOF, this Agreement has been executed by Grantor and by the Trustee in three counterparts, any one of which shall be deemed an original.

_____

[Grantor], GRANTOR

(SEAL)

_____

[Trustee], TRUSTEE

STATE OF _____)

                             SS:

COUNTY OF_____)

On this _____ day of _____ , _____ , before me, a Notary Public, personally appeared [Grantor], the Grantor in the foregoing agreement, and [Trustee], the Trustee in the foregoing agreement ,who are to me known to be the persons described in and who executed the foregoing Agreement, and acknowledged that the persons executed the same as the person's free act and deed.

IN TESTIMONY WHEREOF, I have hereunto set my hand and affixed my official seal the day and year last above written.

_____

Notary Public

The following described assets of Grantor are being transferred to the foregoing trust, subject to all the terms and provisions thereof:

1. All of the tangible personal property of [Grantor] now owned or hereafter acquired, which property is hereby assigned and conveyed to the trust, specifically:.

2. Other property to be transferred to trust by changing title hereto: [bank accts; stock; vehicles; real property].

Appendix D:

Sample Outline of a Will: Do not copy or use without consultation with an attorney. Every person's situation is different.

LAST WILL AND TESTAMENT

of

[Testator]

[Name of Testator and Introduction] I, [Testator] of [County], [State], declare this to be my Last Will and Testament and revoke all other Wills and Codicils heretofore made by me.

ARTICLE I

PAYMENT OF TAXES, DEBTS AND EXPENSES

[Deals with how and what expenses should be paid and the source of those funds]

ARTICLE II

SPECIFIC BEQUESTS AND
DISTRIBUTION OF TANGIBLE PERSONAL PROPERTY

(A) [Makes specific gifts to specific people]

(B) [For real property not specifically given to certain people, that property is given generally to the spouse if that spouse survives , otherwise to somebody else, generally children either to those surviving or per stirpes – by right of representation. Also allows the executor to sell property and distribute proceeds.]

(C) [For tangible and intangible personal property not specifically given to certain people, that property is given generally to the spouse if that spouse survives , otherwise to somebody else, generally children either to those surviving or per stirpes – by right of representation. Also allows the executor to sell property and distribute proceeds.]

ARTICLE III

DISTRIBUTION OF REMAINDER OF PROPERTY

[Residuary clause to catch loose ends. What, how and to whom.]

ARTICLE IV

SPECIAL PROVISIONS

(A)   [Spendthrift provision]

(B)   [No Contest provision]

(C)   [Exercise of Powers]

ARTICLE V

ADMINISTRATIVE POWERS OF PERSONAL REPRESENTATIVE

In addition to their existing authority, and unless this Will provides otherwise, my Personal Representative may:

(A) through (P)   [Grant of powers to executor to perform their duties]

ARTICLE VI

FIDUCIARY PROVISIONS

(A) Appointment of Personal Representative and Guardian.

1.–2.   [Appointment of executor and any Guardians of minor children]

(B) [Waiver of bond.].

(C) Provisions for interpreting Will.

1. [Definition of terms]

2. [The captions of Articles and Paragraphs appearing herein are   for convenience of reference only and shall have no significance in the construction or interpretation of this Will.]

(D) [Authorization to hire professional help and limitations on liability]

(E) [Identification of children.]

I, the Testator, sign my name to this instrument this _____ day of _____, and being first duly sworn, do hereby declare to the undersigned authority that I sign and execute this instrument as my will and that I sign it willingly (or willingly direct another to sign for me), that I execute it as my free and voluntary act for the purposes expressed in the will, and that I am eighteen years of age or older, of sound mind, and under no constraint or undue influence.

_____
[Testator]

We, the witnesses, at the Testator's request, sign our names to this instrument, being first duly sworn, and do hereby declare to the undersigned authority that the Testator signs and executes this instrument as the Testator's will and that the Testator signs it willingly (or willingly directs another to sign for the Testator), and that each of us, in the presence and hearing of the Testator, hereby signs this will as witness to the Testator's signing, and that to the best of our knowledge the Testator is eighteen years of age or older, of sound mind, and under no constraint or undue influence.

_____ of _____
Witness

_____ of _____
Witness

STATE OF _____)

                                          SS:

COUNTY OF_____)

        We, the Testator and the witnesses, respectively, whose names are signed to the attached or foregoing instrument, being first duly sworn, do hereby declare to the undersigned authority that the Testator signed and executed the instrument as the Testator's will and that the Testator had signed willingly (or willingly directed another to sign for the Testator), and that the Testator executed it as the Testator's free and voluntary act for the purposes expressed in the will, and that each of the witnesses, in the presence and hearing of the Testator, and at the request of the Testator, signed the will as witness and that to the best of the witnesses' knowledge the Testator was at that time eighteen years of age or older, of sound mind, and under no constraint or undue influence.

_____

Witness Testator

_____

Witness

Subscribed, sworn to and acknowledged before me by, [Testator], the Testator, and subscribed and sworn to before me by _____ and _____, witnesses, this _____ day of _____.

(Seal)

(Signed)

                                  _____

                                      NOTARY

Appendix E:

Sample Pour-Over Will Clauses

Distribution to trust. I give all the rest of my property to the then acting Trustee of the trust which I created by Trust Agreement dated _____ to be added to and disposed of as a part of that trust.

Alternate distribution provision bypassing trust. Regardless of any contrary provision, if the beneficiaries of any separate trust to which I have left my property under this Will are entitled to receive from the Trustee the entire principal of the trust as soon as it is distributed from my estate to the trust, (as a result of the beneficiary having previously given the Trustee the notice therein provided or because the trust as to such beneficiary has otherwise terminated), then my Personal Representative may make the distribution directly to the beneficiaries to whom and in the same proportions as the Trustee would have been required to make the distribution upon receipt of the property from my Personal Representative.

Appendix F:

Sample Outline of Provisions to Create a Testamentary Trust.

ARTICLE _____

CREATION OF TRUST

[Introduction}

(A) [Division of trust property.]

     1. [Trust A. The first share (to be created only if my spouse, [Spouse], survives me), called "Trust A," shall be in an amount equal to the value of all property to be divided into shares, reduced by the lesser of (i) the maximum amount that will avoid any federal estate tax being due in my estate, and (ii) the maximum amount that will avoid any state death tax being due in my estate. In determining the said amount, any property disclaimed by my spouse shall be disregarded.]

     2. [Trust B. The second share, called "Trust B," shall consist of that property which is not included in Trust A, and shall consist of all the property if my spouse does not survive me.]

(B) [Distribution of Trust A. The Trustee shall distribute Trust A as follows:]

    1. [Distribution during life of spouse.]

        (a)   [Distribution of income to spouse.]

        (b)   [Distribution of principal to spouse.]

    2. [Distribution upon death of spouse.]

        (a) [Spouse's power to appoint trust assets].

        (b) [Distribution of rest of trust assets].

    3. [Marital deduction protective provision for Trust A.]

(C) [Distribution of Trust B].

    1. [Distribution during life of spouse.]

    2. [Distribution following death of spouse.]

        (a) [Provision for living child.]

        (b) [Provision for children of deceased child.]

(D) [Default distribution provisions.]

ARTICLE ____

ALTERNATE PROVISIONS FOR DISTRIBUTION

[Introduction]

(A) [Trust distributions directly to beneficiary.]

(B) [Distribution to other trusts.]

(C) [Retention of distribution to minor.]

(D) [Distribution in the event of divorce.]